LIVE FOR A LIVING

BY BUDDY WAKEFIELD

For Bryan
W/ [G] Love.

And My Special

Sauce,

Buddy Wakefield

A publication of Write Bloody Publishing, Nashville, TN

For more information or to contact:
buddy@buddywakefield.com

Cover image by Chris A'Lurede
www.monstromo.com

Layout by Nathan Warkentin
nrwarkentin@gmail.com

www.writebloody.com

CONTENTS PAGE

* indicates journal entry

INTRODUCTION

There's this gracious intangible thing with lots of names like "Peace," "Love," "God," "Salvation," "Happiness," "Equanimity." Call it anything ya wanna call it, but everybody – whether they admit it or not – wants it. It doesn't speak or move or invade or deny or convince. It just is, like air. Exactly like air. Whenever I find I've trailed off too far from my awareness of it, I know that I can write my way back inside. It's why I write. When it's time to heal and bring chaotic thoughts to resolve, I write. It's so much the answer for me that my body wants to tell you too. So I perform what I write.

You are reading the words of a sucker, a sucker for solution, and catharsis, and clarity, revival, redemption, and release. Taking the time to write my way back Home, through any given space that might slip between me and Happiness, is my life's work. And for a moody guy like me, there is much work to be done.

But be a little leery of people like me in my current state. Despite my proper intensions and inherent good will, I am addicted to revival and redemption and release. In order to be revived one must first be exhausted. In order to be redeemed one first has to fail. In order to be released we have to first be trapped. Inspiration can turn into a tricky cycle if we're not careful. Sometimes I'm ignorant to the rest of my elements when I show so much preference to inspiration, like massages, or waterslides. Those things are expensive.

Upon fully realizing the circle I've been allowing myself to run in, I wrote myself the following garbled note:

...so don't come to me, poet, with your ink and your holy experience
sittin' there all raw pretending not to be,
all that vulnerability bubblin' under yer surface
actin' unconscious of how awkward you make things at the dinner table.
You scathe your observations, then bathe 'em then
Call 'em all out on stages

reaffirming that you're right about a thing or two
because you didn't get enough confidence
from the people who swiped you through school.
Approval junky.
Pressure cooker.
Smoke stacker
steady whistles
speed tears streamin'
exhausted from excuses
still hopin' we can hover on
holy
when you're finally finished claiming

THERE IS NOTHING WRONG
THERE'S NOT ANYTHING WRONG
IT'S JUST YOU AND ME, BUDDY
AND A TICKING TIME BOMB!

THERE
Right THERE
inside the lie,
the one you've been telling yourself
the entire time you were dying to walk away,
Heart Wormer,
Mr. Self-Murder,
walk away.
Still yourself.

Then, after tubehopping through alotta thoughts that night about how much due credit I'm capable of withholding from myself (e.g. I've never really walked around pretending there's nothing wrong), I interviewed my strengths and ended with a series of statements:

You get the feelin' that one day you're just gonna snap?

No, I don't.
Anybody else in here feel like a ticking time bomb?
No, it's just something interesting to say.

I'm no longer interested in watching you rise from the falls you keep taking in vain
just for a reason to stand.

My favorite thing to do is see things clearly.

I ain't sayin' revival, redemption and release are unnatural or bad, I'm just sayin'
that when you're tired of the rise and the fall and the ensuing circle,
walk away.
Still yourself.

Nothing more or less happened
than what happened.

This book is for those of us who've experienced the moment
and did not need any other answer than exactly what happened.

While others are losing trust that it is possible,
it is still possible.

The pace of my career up to the summer of 2006 was still manageable enough
that I was able to answer most of the emails from people who support my art. At a
certain point, though, after Sage Francis and his fans also put their trust in my CD,
Run on Anything, I began receiving more messages from folks than I was able to
answer with quality of thought (even though I still had time to at least read them),
so I made this journal entry on my website:

Inward Bound
July 6, 2006

Spread me out and run highway lines up my throat. Tire eyes. Sleepless. I feel like a prick when I don't answer to each person individually, because I see you. It feels good to know you noticed and that you give a shit. Sometimes I'm juggling too many skyscrapers on full plates to respond. It don't mean I'm not thanking you directly from the goose bump in my heartbeat. Much Love & Respect, Bed

It should become obvious that regardless of the titles throughout this book, anything with a date is a journal entry and anything with only a title only is an intended poem. Journal entries have been edited for grammar, succinctness and coherency, not so much for creative writing. I wanted to leave who I was in the moment intact. Despite whoever I claim to be in the varying signatures after each journal entry, it's me.

There are an immeasurable number of individuals to whom I owe thanks for contributing to my ongoing account of waking up, so I will herein stick to a very select few who have most immediately affected my career and made this book possible:

My mother, the Guitar Repair Woman, who personifies the words *won't give up.*

My producer, Jon Berardi, who happens to be about as close to a perfect friend that anyone could ask for.

My publisher, Derrick Brown, for being my creative role model, for filling me with laughter, and for showing me the good that comes from not trying to be perfect.

Sage Francis, for believing in me enough to chuck me way the fuck outta my comfort zone into a genre I would otherwise have never fully experienced, and gifting me with immeasurable experience and exposure.

Ani DiFranco and her mother, Elizabeth, for grace unspoken, and for granting me the opportunity to see all my delusions of rock star grandeur come to life.

And to Remond Liesting for revealing the friendship and Love I aspire to. Though any given circumstance can be a catalyst for "The Butterfly Effect," Remond's wings seem to have caused my greatest tidal waves. I would say he is the reflection and teacher I trust more than anyone in my life, but he taught me how digressive it is to speak in superlatives.

I feel very fortunate indeed that life has led me here. Welcome. Thanks very much for taking the time to support my work. Means the world to me to get to do what I love for a living. Hopefully you've arrived here in an effort to see more, with new eyes, and not just in terms of how naked everything can get. Let's try doin' this openly human, together, adjust the tuners, go vulnerable (big symptom of individuality), cards on the table, big me big you.

Confidentiality does not exist here, just respect.

With Much Hope and Excitement for Right Now,

Buddy Wakefield

WHEN YA GET BACK HOME

NOVEMBER 27, 2005

It's 5am Sunday morning. Just woke up from a nightmare. I was parked on the side of a neighborhood street with two cop cars that kept shifting their parked positions around me. There was a pick-up truck parked ahead of the rest of us. All four parked cars were on varying sides of the street.

There was someone in my passenger's seat telling me to do things like turn off my bright lights, take my foot off the accelerator, things to keep the cops from gettin' out, comin' over and effin' with me.

It was dark and I was paranoid. I've always resented the fact that when a cop drives by I feel paranoid instead of protected.

I realized we were parked on a street, across from the house where an old friend from high school lived. Said friend was quite likely the most impacting person in my first twenty years other than my mother.

I did not look over to see the voice of reason in my passenger's seat but I'm sure it was the man in the mirror.

My paranoia balled up like a sweaty fist. Don't take your eyes off the road or the speedometer or the gauges, and *hold steady*. I kept telling myself these things. But we were still parked.

The passenger in my car finally encouraged me to pull out and go around the cops and the pick-up truck and just drive. The truck turned on its headlights and pulled out behind me as I passed it. I grew very fearful. At the end of the street I came up on the stop sign too fast, braking just [cross] hairs from the perpendicular traffic. I worried how the truck would not have enough time to stop before ramming into me from behind.

No damage. I signaled proper and turned left. So did the truck.

Stop following.

Leave me alone.

In a fraction of a second and a fracture of light, the truck threw on its high beams just before I hit some kind of thick unseen slick in the road. My car spun around fast, screeching, whiplash, stopped, stillness. The entire time, of course, death was upon me and – just as I suspected that the moment would murder me – I woke up with the man in the mirror asking why I did not for one second realize that every single person in the dream was intending good on me.

***

I had just finished a mini-tour in the Northeast, had flown from Buffalo to Atlanta, and was awaiting my connection flight in a packed airport restaurant. There were two older men sitting at the bar next to me with their computers open, talking about which companies to buy out. Their immediate net gain on any given purchase would be no less than $300,000.00. They were impressed with themselves (or maybe that was me), and trying to be professional as opposed to giggly about having the upper hand in their situations. Their puffy chests were invasive. They spoke loud enough for others to hear about all that money and status. Both they and I had ordered the same meal, which – of course – required sauce.

They did not touch their sides of sauce. So, as they volleyed job-specific terms and kept their backs straight, my inner classicist kicked in. I (poorly dressed and lookin' a little rugged from travel) leaned over, pointed at their sides of sauce and said, "You kids gonna eat your sauce?" I said it in the tone of Big Me - little you. I said it so they couldn't necessarily tell, but I was looking for one of them to be weak about it.

What the hell was that? My way of condescending to two people I believed probably talked down to everyone around them on a regular basis. Was I trying to get back at them on behalf of poor people everywhere, or was I entertaining myself? I was filled with such judgment that they were just another pair of corporate sluts. I didn't even think to consider how they might have been funding a school for altruists, or lepers. Realistically, my instincts probably weren't far off, but who the hell am I to create such catty animosity? And why the hell would I want to?

They gladly gave me one of their sauces.

***

I walked out of the restaurant bar and headed toward my gate. The first thing I noticed at a glance was two different men in conversation, both unkempt in sloppy jeans. One had an untrimmed mustache, worked hands and an aged windbreaker. He says to the other, "You get a real toughness growing up in the navy…"

As I passed them and giggled, visions of navy uniforms in mind, I cranked my neck around to size them up, to get a better look at the supposed tough guy. The back of his windbreaker read: GIRLS SWIM TEAM.

I pegged his stupidity for a moment, then recognized it as my own.

***

I was a good Texas son for Thanksgiving. There was only one day when my mom and stepdad and stepbrother and I would all have a whole day off together. I was ready to embrace the week with a great attitude and went for the last thing any of them would expect… I suggested we all go get family portraits! I was hoping for the old school Olan Mills type situation… but, even better: SEARS.

It was a wonderful time. Our photographer had a wonderful time. We had a wonderful time. We were dressed in variations of red, white and blue, no less. I felt appreciation for the folks. The pictures came out perfect. We ate at the aquarium in Kemah that night, raced remote-controlled boats, strolled, saw sunset.

I worked out every morning to start the day. Filled up Mom's gas tank. My stepbrother and I went out a couple nights together for the first time in our lives, had drinks, talked eye to eye. I had gifts for my stepfather's side of the family that I bought because I really wanted to, and felt joy picking them out. They had always thought of me on the holidays. There was even a dinner date with an old friend. We had gone to her senior Prom together and had watched each other grow up through a phase or two. We met in Baytown, where I lived from 6th-12th grade, mostly.

***

I drove into Baytown four hours early to have a look around, observe changes, visit folks, and remember back to where I slaughtered the inner lamb. The moment I crossed over the bridge, that familiar smell of copper/diesel/leather/sulfur/sex seeped in, caked on, and all my insecurities came with it, highlighted, pumped my stomach.

Everybody gives me reasons why their town will be bombed first.
It's a souped-up sense of self-importance...

Everybody's got a story. So does everybody's town. Most of us pretend we had it the best or worst through some aspect of where we were brought up. It's foolish pride. I get it, so I'm not vying for bragging rights when I tell you that Baytown is a place where mostly packs of wolves take pride in being the worst of the worst; a place where no child – if presented with the facts – would ever choose to grow up.

Despite all the greatness still in my friends who continue to live there, and the good-hearted people who taught me good-heartedness, Baytown itself is an infection. As well as having one of the largest ports in the world (6th), 75% of the town is owned by Exxon/Mobile. Formerly in the Guinness Book of World Records, Baytown boasts the largest refinery in North America (now second in the world, behind a refinery in Scotland). But it doesn't end at just one of the world's largest refineries... Collectively, it is part of a mammoth chain of Texas towns that cannot be stopped except by law of nature. Refineries spill out of Baytown in every direction covering the 45-minute drive down to the Gulf of Mexico, across to Houston, in every direction. Exxon/Mobil, BP/Amoco, Motiva [Shell/Texaco (Equilon)], Monsanto, Crown Central, Lyondell Citgo, Brown & Root (Halliburton), Valero, Total Petrochemicals, Atofina, Haltermann Products, Premcor, Marathon Ashland, Chevron... Smoke stacks as far as the eye can see. When ya grow up breathing the stink, watching the sky squat overhead just suckin' it up, it's easy to become it. Iron lung.

It has always seemed strange to me when the root of the problem is where the least number of people act to heal the situation (e.g. Hitler's Germany). Maybe they're too close, hopped up on co-dependency and fear, fooled by the cattle drive. It's a harmful environment to say the least, but they will defend it to the death. The bonds I held growing up in Texas were incredible, and we took great pride in the shit we endured, the drugs we absorbed, the fights we created, the uninformed rebellion, and in the deep limits we imposed on ourselves.

Combined with the Houston smog is scorching heat and humidity, biting insect and critter manifestations I do not know how to name, toxic dumping with untold side-effects, awful smell, rampant misinformation among the foolishly prideful (*many* of whom *still* tout rebel flags and use N-words with zero consideration of their snowball effect). There's the far-right conservative base, the racial tension, the embrace of trashy attitudes, the creativity-smothering machismo, the blind group-think... Baytown fed my hostility in all its dismal, violent and life-sucking forms.

As I sat at a neighborhood pool hall, hearing all the updates and rundowns from and about my close classmates and childhood friends, I'll admit to the heartbreak. I'll admit to giving myself some extra credit for the kick-ass choices I've made. I'll admit to thanking my constantly-changing lucky stars for ever leaving that place with so much hope and a smile in the first place.

It was incredible to hear and learn of the ones who turned (or are turning) out to be content, happy, alive. Some are still there in Baytown, and their own experiences outshine any narrow blanket statements I can make...

***

Finished "Knulp" by Hermann Hesse and have started Ken Wilbur's "A Theory of Everything."

The best part of my trip was petting sting rays under the Kemah Aquarium with my mother and Jeffrey, my brother.

Great Day Ahead, Hoss

The following was written as an introduction to the poem My Town. I didn't know it would be so well-received as a performance piece able to stand on its own. I wrote this intro in September of 2006 so I could banter with audiences then seamlessly start the actual poem "My Town" during live performances. Now I'm able to use both the intro and the poem at shows individually or as a whole.

MY TOWN INTRO

My town is cute
like a bumper sticker
like when Christians sport **POWER OF PRIDE** bumper stickers.
What is it you don't understand about pride being a deadly sin?

My town is cute like **GOD BLESS AMERICA** bumper stickers.
Judging by our excessive luxuries, those stickers really work.
Now if we can just get God to bless the whole world.

Alix Olsen's bumper sticker reads **I LOVE MY COUNTRY.**
I JUST THINK WE SHOULD START SEEING OTHER PEOPLE.
But my town doesn't see other people.
We're just too cute
like the difference between what we say and what we do
like the fact that violence in any form
is sanctioned by the government as criminal or insane
unless they're the ones who commit it.

My town is cute like people who still shop at Wal-Mart and claim to be patriotic.
Stop it.

My town is cute in the way we worry about the gays
fuckin' up our family values and the sanctity of marriage
yet we still let our children watch television shows like *Wife Swap,*
*The Bachelor, Who Wants to Marry a Millionaire, American Idol*atry
and *Fox News.*

My town is so cute that – check this out –
once, six years ago,
there were some brown people *(boogity boogity),*
they attacked two of our tallest buildings
and killed a shitload of our innocent citizens,
kinda like we did
in Guatemala, Nicaragua, Panama, El Salvador,
Tanzania, Mozambique, Vietnam, Afghanistan,
Hiroshima, Philippines, Kosovo, Bolivia,
Angola, Argentina, Brazil, Chile, Dresden,
Dominican Republic, Cuba, Haiti, Indonesia,
East Timor, Cambodia, Iraq, (what the fuck
are we doing with Israel?)
and my cute town pretends we never saw it [or had it] coming
so in a perpetual attempt to save cute face
we've waged a war on terror about as effective as the war on drugs.
My town is cute when we wage these wars in the name of God.

As many as 20% of the polar bears on the Northern Ice Cap are hermaphrodites
due to PCBs being dumped into the ocean.
You won't hear about that shit on the news because it's too cute,
like a wolf giving birth through its penile canal *(True).*

My town is cute like a 300lb tumor manifesting hair and teeth inside of it
grown from the body of a 210 pound agoraphobic woman,
cute like competitive poetry, the history of Scientology, plastic surgery,
and refined sugars, cute
like a man swallowing an 8-ball of cocaine
then jumping from a 5-story building to escape police,
getting up and running away from it all.

Y'all, *this*
this is a true story:

The first time My Town saw the sky
it sucker punched us in the throat
left us breathless
said, "I'm gonna keep you awake some nights
without touching you
you'll make it up, *the pain,*
you always do."

I wrote most of the poem My Town on a train from Nuremburg, Germany to Rot-terdam, Netherlands inspired from reading Derrick Brown's book, "Born in the Year of the Butterfly Knife." I owe the development of the tea-bagging line to Michael Bongiorno.

MY TOWN

The first time my town saw the sky
it sucker punched us in the throat
left us breathless
said, "I'm gonna keep you awake some nights
without touching you
you'll make it up, the pain,
you always do."

Now my town only buys drowsy formula sky.
Otherwise it gets too big, the sky,
like when we were three
before we realized:

    We have balls.
    The sky does not.
    Therefore, we have bigger balls than the sky.

Please
do not talk to us about being tea-bagged
by upside down hot air balloons.

Where rational conversation and big pictures are concerned
we have no time for getting wrapped up.
We are not little presents for your sky.
We are just right.
Far right.

And cute
like 3-year-olds,
like the book about bunny suicides,
cute like Old Yeller just 'fore he got shot in the rabies
(a good actor, that dog).

My town was born way off the mark.
Sometimes we see it coming, the mark,
so we shoot it with spit wads or
precision-guided phallic symbols.

Every time there is talk of war
people give me reasons why their town
will be bombed first.
It's a souped-up sense of self importance, bucko.
Everybody knows my town will be bombed first
because once
we planned the construction of a nuclear power plant
right here in the same fields where our military children
now carry out covert orders to keep the word *dumb* alive.

Christianity has a hard time workin' here,
makes us believe that even when we are alone
someone is watching us and judging us.
Now we're all narcissists.
We have a habit of giving other people's gifts to ourselves.

But at least our children still get their confidence booster shots,
while our fathers perform voice reduction surgery
to keep our pleas for help mime-sized,
while our mothers are bending infinity in half
so that our families can continue to talk in circles,
while we all burn our tongues when we drink hot cocoa

for the same reason everybody here wants to hug the ocean,
because it's just *so much*.

My town knows that there is something *so big* inside of all of us
we have to suck
just to distract you from being directly overwhelmed by our *real* power,
the kind of power that makes you smile.
Everybody knows that smiling is for little girls, the gays
and certain kinds of fish
who are smiling by accident.

The shortcuts my town has taken
have saved us so little time
gotten us so far ahead of ourselves
we've actually fallen behind.
Would have been better off learning to herd turtles
into bomb shelters, on a moment's notice,
giggling at the fact that we will all now die
and it'll have happened so fast
we will have never been anything
but really cute
like our three-year-olds
who use folding chairs
to beat lambs within inches of their lives.

My town is inches tall.
It's why the sky looks down on us
wants to tell us something
like   *grow up*
or   *reach up*
or   *look up and watch me winking.*
      I'm trying to talk to you.

The Earth is traveling at 66,641 mph around the sun.
It simultaneously rotates on itself at over 1,000 mph.
My town? Yeah,
it's having some trouble sleeping.

BURN DART THE BONE YARD

JANUARY 01, 2006

Scoop: Lighting fireworks was a tradition born in the Far East as a way of scaring off ghosts and bringing in the New Year free of evil spirits.

After what I saw last night, Rotterdam should be just about out of poltergeists. This city got saged; looked like it was jacked up on stampede dust, shouted and showered pyrotechnic from every angle. The Dutch, they were driving out demons last night and it was beautiful.

"...and I see you ridin' a big red horse, and you're drivin' them horses, whippin' 'em. And they're spittin' and frothin' all along the mouth, and they're comin' right at us. And I see the future. There's no death..."
— Mallory Knox, Natural Born Killer

Remond and I watched from our third floor balcony where we have views of the North, South and East.

At the risk of spewing superlative, I've never seen such a massive and lasting parade of works, popped and drizzled in from all sides; up from the street, down from the roof, over from the skyscrapers, out of the canal, along the street car tracks, off the balconies, between the entry ways, through the building blocks, over the rooftops, tricked-out and loud.

Fireworks are legal here. Everyone is allowed to shoot them, *in* the city. But it's not just the fireworks that are legal; so's the fire...

I mean bangs had been banging for over two days, a slow build to the New Year. I'd already learned from being here at New Year's last year that I should be wary when approaching young groups of shit-eatin' grins. It's good times in these parts to chuck a firecracker under the feet of somebody you don't know.

24

I was not a victim. I kept my game face on. You know, the one that says, "Throw a firecracker at me and I will meat cleaver you."

There seems to be a fine line between bombs and firecrackers in Holland. The firecrackers here go above and beyond the call of bang duty, seem to compete with each other for sonic boom status. After two days of these sporadic noise surprises, once the morning of December 31st hits, explosions around town ramp up to a pretty steady pace.

By midday, the noise thickens and we could pass for battlefield. Cue the whistlers.

Within a couple hours of midnight the bubble bursts and gusts of gunpowder clouds roll around in smoke sheets covering the city. We inhaled them.

Re and I had started celebrating with drink around 6pm. I'm a lightweight since before the fast that I did just before the Vipassana retreat. I don't drink much anymore. We ate dinner around 11pm to curb the early tipsy I was slurrin.'

By 11:40pm I had resigned from the idea of staying up till 1am just for the sake of going out downtown and entering chaos. I was content to lay around until midnight, when Re and I could chill and watch fireworks from the bed out the window, then sleep.

By 11:55pm the works were in full effect and there was a kick-ass show right outside our bedroom window facing West, surprisingly close.

At midnight the lights and sounds split the night wide open.

Re doesn't build things up. There was no warning. He doesn't like to give people expectations, so I didn't really know what was comin.'

Here's the thing: I was here last year. We were standing in downtown Rotterdam in the thick of the noise and smoke, but were walled by giant buildings, and I was unable to grasp the scope of what was taking place around me. About thirty minutes into that thunder last year, we had walked to a bar that would open at 1am like the rest of the city does on New Year's Eve. I didn't know what we were missing last year.

Anyhow, my experience with the fireworks of Rotterdam was way different this time around.

Once the exploding lights started taking up more of my view than the open sky did, I hopped out of bed to see how it all looked from the balcony on the other side of our place.

Second wind! We threw on some warm gear, then went back to the balcony where we stayed through at least a six-pack and a cup of homemade hot cocoa. WHAT?!

It's not just that it was beautiful up there, it's that it didn't stop.

Just below us, folks from the building across the street were in the middle of the road, burning off firework after firework, aiming roman candles, blocking traffic, lighting packs of "million bangs" (massive stretches of bundled firecrackers that crack ears hard for minutes at a time).

At least an hour into the finale Re laughed and said, "So many good intensions" (with reference to the tradition of driving out evil spirits).

Keep in mind that we were *in* the city. There's no country spacing or scattered houses. We are stacked one on top of the other for miles, so it was a total surprise when – as if I wasn't impressed enough by the way Rotterdam lights up a New Year – the neighbors decided to get their Christmas tree, place it on the middle of the streetcar tracks, and set the mufugger on fire.

"Re! What the eff is that? Is that cool?" I was kinda trippin' on the what-ifs.

Re looked over our balcony, didn't flinch: "Oh, yeah, a freedom fire."

"Is that legal?"

"Yup."

A cop even passed by the kid while the kid was lighting it, slowed down, kept going. Don't get me wrong, the cops are just as much dicks here as they are anywhere else, but there's not much he could do... it's legal to start a bonfire in the middle of the street during a celebration like this.

So, by this point Rotterdam was still repeatedly giving birth to quintuplet spar-kle concerts from every angle, the city was completely caked in smoke (which seemed to carry the vibe of incense), there was a Christmas tree blazing on the tracks where our streetcar was to pass, and another fire was being started down by the old folks' home (which literally looks like the front end of a half-drowned Titanic that got bricked and now oversees our neighborhood).

About this time, one very focused and maniacal neighbor was setting off anti-climactic bottle rocket after anti-climactic bottle rocket, which made him completely slow motion compared to the blitz of energy around him. He had found an empty firework tube, was placing one cheap rocket at a time inside, lighting it and running away as if it would hurt him should he get too close... Did I mention he was in the middle of the street?

There was no sign of the action stopping any time soon. The locals appeared pretty calm about all this. Having already decided what things I would gather from our apartment before it burned to the ground, I was keepin' it cool and enjoying myself... until a car caught on fire.

"Re!"

Re was making hot cocoa.

"Re! There's a car on fire!"

Because of the distance from our balcony to the parking area, it was hard to tell whether or not that was our car on fire.

"Yeah, Bud?"

"Re, dude, COME HERE!" He doesn't have the fastest reaction time. Okay, truth be told, he kind of has to be asked to react.

Re made it out to the balcony and confirmed, "Oohp, yeap, our car's on fire."

"Is that our car?!!"

"Yeah." Okay, ya just gotta know the way Re speaks and simultaneously laughs the sentiment of "so what" at the same time.

The car's horn sounded off for at least two minutes before burning out. The insides were being completely gutted by fire and the wind had given the flame intimidating height as it punched through the back window. Before long, the entire car was engulfed.

Re went back into the kitchen to finish making cocoa.

"Re, should we maybe do something?!"

"Hold on!" he shouted from the kitchen.

He brought out the cocoa, then strolled back inside to grab the binoculars. It wasn't our car. It was the car next to our car. I told Re that the camera with all our pictures are in the car so that maybe he would have a reason to react. Sure, he was a little disappointed, but...

The fire truck finally arrived (NOT because we called them; sometimes Re just likes to leave it up to the universe to work shit out, ya know).

The fire was fought and there was no damage to our car. Unbelievable. Thank goodness all the snow melted yesterday and left everything wet.

There was no definitive point when the show ended. The people of Rotterdam launched light for at least an hour and a half. As for the noise works, we can still hear those goin' off intermittently even right now, 18 hours later.

My plane leaves in a couple days. It's been an incredible month. Before I get too sappy here in public about how much I'm gonna miss Re in the space between (and our little jaguar Dachshunds, Thomas and Edward), I'll just sign off.

May you find happiness in 2006.

Resolution, You
P.S. I posted the above entry last night before bed. This morning Re found our car also gutted by fire.

FLOCKPRINTER

Flockprinting is an aggressive electrostatic action
using severe heat
to force finely chopped fibers
onto patterns of fabric
ultimately resulting
in soft touch.

When they told You that this was Your assignment
You flockprinted straitjackets and suits of armor
so I asked if You wanted to trade jobs
because damn, Baby,
that
is poetry.

And yeah, these arms fell backwards when ya did it
chest outstretched
open to the way You palms-up turn me
I knew You'd be good.
I just didn't know how good.

Even before we met,
when the assignment was to draw words
with their own literal meanings
I would write out each letter of the word LOVE
using winning halves of wishbones, melted Crayons
and the toe-tips of the great dancers who've quit dancing
because I don't give up on shit like that.
I always knew I'd find You.

Even before we met,
when the assignment was to partner up in ice water

and keep our heads above it,
I'd watch boys with girls
take the shallow end of the 8th grade like
suckerfish
swapping skin deep aquarium air tubes
trying to make each other's shivers fit.
We don't swim that way.
Never gonna.

Flockprinter
You have been a long time comin'
and the clouds have rolled You in slowly.
But I ain't mad at the upshot sky.
Rain,
it's my lucky number.
It's the author of release.
It taught me monsters are easy to come by
so I went out and found the beast
before we met
when the assignment was to incomplete myself
with sad songs and recycled insults,
when I was spun out, eyes bagged
teeth fist-first in lust and considering Jesus.
You were there.
You have been the whole journey
and I ain't got nothin' against goin' home
to You, Flockprinter.

You look good in yer tidal wave,
toe-to-toe with the mean blue moon,
head raised up like a lighthouse.
You are buttercups spraying out the mouths of doves,
fireworks stuck in the air.

You're a freestanding landing pad
held together by choir claps.
You're a god not afraid to walk with the saviors
who ride monkeys around on their backs
kicking up mercury
spreading upward openly,
carrying breath
well.

You're an18-stringed guitar heart sparkin'
off of roots dancing out of the river's edge.
You walk like a free country
with an affinity for thick skin.
You live
humming to the tune of let loose like a railway
banging through the middle of Novocain,
an open-winded underwater fire escape.

Flockprinter,
You have, now are, and always will be
my reflection of individuality
carried out by the acoustic drift
of a snowflake
livin' with a fingerprint.

And I
am rumble motion jawbone
waterlogged with ink spots
smiling ear to ear
armed with backbone and busted zoo gates
promising You
from the bottom of my harmonica pocket
forever,

You will never have another lonely holiday.

Even now,
where the assignment is to live without a destination,
I end up with You and the rain, released
both
flockprinting stars
between me and the beast.

TWIN BLUE HIGHWAY HEAD

MARCH 13, 2007

It's 4:46am in the Seattle airport
waiting on a plane.
No sleep yet.

I am paying close attention to people
and typing into my phone.
Cursor.
Cursor.
Cursor.
Cursor.
Cursor.
We are on orange alert.

David Lynch wrote a movie called *This Morning*.
And I'm in it.
A lot.
In the men's room I walked in on a somewhat-retarded pale kid standing confused
under the fluorescent light in the mirror, using his jaw to pull his jaw off. Didn't
work, so he mashed his lips into each other and around. He was pretending to not
be startled by my entry. He was slow to the startle. He felt so goddamned sad.

There is one thin single-spaced exceedingly long line for expensive bagels and
coffee, but hardly anyone else in the airport. They're all just standing there, three
gates long, mooing, quietly. I'm loud hungry inside but the thought of standing
with them makes no sense to me.

To get here
I ran down the escalator by myself
without looking up at that stupid window
from where people wave goodbye.

Today I believe in ghosts. Again.
Cursor.
Cursor.
Cursor.
I've found as much love for airports as I have for myself.
And as much hate.

Synchronicity just kicked in on cue (i.e. the guy next to me dials his phone and says to someone at the other end, "This is a voice from your past.").

I miss his voice.
I miss him so goddamn much.

Fluorescent Fixture, Flicker

GIANT SAINT EVERYTHING

There were days I wanted out.
But then You would go and do things
like dive into the Vancouver ocean,
big brilliant cliché poem that You are,
water rolling off Your back
as You swam toward a sunset
that hung like a sacred recipe painted
all the way around Your holy head.

And then there were the ways You watched me
moving back into my cave where the wheels turn,
same wheels that drove You off.
I should have told You
before talking in terms of Forever
that any given day wears me out and works me sour,
that there are nights when the sky is so clear
I stand obnoxious underneath it
begging for the stars to shoot at me
just so I can feel at Home.

What's left of You now is a shrine
built from the pieces I kept of Your presence,
Your incredible stretch of presence.
It sits in Our room like a sandpiper
cross-legged and crying,
remembering the night we met
and the day You left, and the Light
shifting in between.
By the side of it stands a picture of the poem where I promised,
"You will never have another lonely holiday."

The words "I Promise" and "Forever"
begged me not to use them
but sometimes I don't listen to God,
so You can imagine how much it hurt
to let Your last birthday pass
with no word. On August 3rd
You weren't the only one comin' up lonesome.

Listen, if I had to make a list
of everything everywhere
- and I mean everything… everywhere -
the very last to-do on that infinite list of
every – single – thing – would be – to hurt You,
so I need You to know
that in an attempt to keep my promise
I did write a letter to You on Your birthday.

It was covered in stickers of flock-printed stars,
choir claps, and a bonfire of buttercups stuck in the air,
but when I finally drew enough courage
to send You all the Love in the World
my hand snapped off in the mailbox
from clenching.

It was returned to me with a gospelstitch, a hope stamp
and a note etched into the palm I had to pry open
with the pressure of pitching doves
reminding me
we agreed to let each other go.

There is a point when tears don't work
to wash things away anymore.
Grabbing for breath has now broken my fingers.

I miss You so much some days
that I beg for the airplane to crash
with just enough time in the freefall
for scribbling "I Love You" across my chest.
That way – when they find my burning breast plate –
they will tell You how the very last thing I did with my life
was call out Your name.

Arnold Remond Liesting

I know Your momma didn't raise a sissy
so it's best if I believe
that You've bounced back and been born again
but, Baby,
in the bottom left corner of dreams
in the dark spot
where it gets windy and hollow
I can still see you flailing,
eating knuckle cake,
full torque and tender,
heart pounding from being pulled under,
feet bleeding from bracing for endings,
tongue dying to curse Forever
because promises murder us backwards
when people like me don't keep them.

And sure, we all deserve absolution,
but especially You. You and Faith,
You've got the same hungerpunch, same song
still rising off the watertrain running through the laws
of a moon dead set on daylight
digging marbles from the trees
of a Love not scared to make no sense

still monkey enough to see
the same devastating reason for living this life:
My Giant
Saint
Everything.

I Promise You.
Forever.

These words have buckled my lips
so far back to the beginning
that I am now only allowed Today.
So today, from my snap-chested heart spraying
fully flying
sending out the birds,
today I stop believing in words.
Today all my visions reverted blurs
like the night We saw the Light
and I could not shut up

but I swear I was feelin' silence.

DYING TO LIVE IN 90 SECONDS

MAY 31, 2005

She said, "When I fly in airplanes I practice dying.
If a plane falls from that far up no one's gonna live.
I figure there's about 90 seconds when everyone on the plane knows
they're gonna die.
So I practice being friends with myself
in 90-second bursts."

"I fly a lot," I tell her, "10 days a month sometimes."

"You must be good at dying by now."

Nonstop voicemail from God lately.

Go soak up the sun and be tickled.

Diver, Gently

After a many-month stint of being hard on myself for not writing as much as I felt I should be, Tim Sanders, on a walk around Greenlake in Seattle, reminded me that I wasn't gonna pour out a satisfying poem every time I sat down to type. He told me to just go write and not be afraid of writing something that sucks. "Gandhi's Autobiography" and "Bedrooms and Battlescars" happened that night. Though far better as performances and off the page, I like how they both turned out.

GANDHI'S AUTOBIOGRAPHY

Gandhi's autobiography is on my pillow.
I put it there every morning after making my bed
so I'll remember to read it before falling asleep.
I've been reading it for 6 years.
I'm on Chapter 2.

Gary Necci gave me a book when he left my house one time.
I don't remember the name of it exactly
but I think it was called something like
"Kid, You Are Seriously Co-dependent."
He thought I might wanna flip through and learn about that.
I feel like it's more important to finish Gandhi's autobiography first.

I keep forgetting to put *focus* on my to-do list.

I keep forgetting to wander and have fun.

I know I'm transparent
but my insecurities are in all the right places
so go ahead
have a look.

When I was a child I would chase my babysitter around the house
viscerally sounding out the end of the letter *L*.

lllllllLLL
…llll

Have another look.

When will we own ourselves completely?
Tell me what it is you want me to own
and I will take it.
Damaged goods?
You bet.
Hit or miss?
No doubt about it.
Misses important social cues?

Yes,
I do.

I'm dirty underneath the light
pale on the backside of my bright
and feel a little bit stupid about learning a language when I see God
because that guy…
so fast.

My best friend can speak six languages.
I still get excited that English took hold.
Sometimes I don't feel like I'm doing my part on this planet.

Sometimes I read without paying attention
hoping everything will just sorta sink in so that
if I ever need the answers – like on a test –
my subconscious will somehow pull through for me.

I talk too much.
If you see me being quiet
don't ask what's wrong.
I'm just practicing.

I often wonder if anyone died because of
the pencil I handed to a prisoner at San Quentin.
He stuck it in his pocket.

The point is:
there are things wrong with us.
There are things wrong with me.

But I do have the ability to split epiphanies with my face on demand.
Hold me like a birthmark,
awkward if you have to.
I wander,
so if you lose me,
don't worry.

After the big tsunami
the only structure still standing in the wiped-out village of Malacca
was a statue of Mahatma Gandhi.
I wanna be able to stand like that.
Even after getting gargled and spanked
and spit out by God,
I wanna know that I don't have to fall
every time the sky opens up like a coin return

to change me
with its pudgy black fingers
tracing lines on maps
drawing circles around my blood
to show the scars here
in the shape of Gandhi on my pillow,
to show that I have been here before
and this is *not* the last time I've seen the light.

BEDROOMS AND BATTLESCARS

As best as I can remember
this is how it happened...

There was a tree in the bottom corner of a corn field
where I hid from people who lived inside my house.
I called them step-sisters and -fathers
but they were monsters
holding out for light.
They were people who did not know what they were holding out for.
They didn't intend to be so beastly and wounded.
They wanted to cross over into the way I wander
but they could not find me,
and I paid for that.

In 1974 I was born.
The next three years were a bit of a blur,
understandably so,
though my mother has repeatedly reminded me
that I was a loud baby.
I wobbled and sucked my thumb
marveled and opened up,
crapped my pants cute as the next kid,
and my cheeks
could be used for sailing.

But in 1978 my mom's car broke down.
We were brutally rescued by a truck driver for eight years.
He had the hell inside of him.
Rug burn.
I know because he pulled me across the floor.

One day my mom decided it was not okay anymore that
he kept falling into other women's va-hoo-hoos
so we left him, realizing
we had not actually been rescued all them years ago.

In those days
I jumped six feet from my light switch to my bed
in order to avoid the hands of anything underneath it.
There are still dents in my shins
because I didn't always hit the mattress.

Bedrooms and battle scars
both keep well in the dark.
Hard dark.
In the sunken-eyed section of a nightmare
paved with uppercuts
and heart sparks
spark plugs and fist-first
release.

I'd fall in love with you
if you would beat these people out of me.

THE RAMA VERSE

AUGUST 22, 2005

Lots of Buddys ago, while I was acting as president of The Christian Cowboys Friends and Fellowship Rodeo Association for a year in college (if only I were joking), a preacher told me about Rama Verses.

A Rama Verse is any passage in the Bible or elsewhere, congruent and honest enough to shotgun chills through my spine and open my eyes that much more, like the first time I read Romans 3:23. A Rama Verse is a passage that stands true in the heart of the reader, holds up the mirror, talks to the spirit, shouts out the truth.

"Mama We're All Crazy Now" by Quiet Riot just came on the radio.
I would be lying if I didn't tell you that it hit me like Rama.
I'm open to counseling.

Special shout out to my campers from Stanford University who I bumped into at Seattle's Hempfest yesterday. You both looked beautiful and slightly off-kilter, same way a chuckle works. I hope y'all gathered lots of literature on the profound benefits and practical applications of hemp while having a good time. It's too important a resource to be mistaken for novelty.

Come on, Feel the Noise,
Edmund Aslan

AIR HORN

And when the rain
dropped into us
another song
we went along
we played a long
tambourine
shaped like a tree
made out of bones
I shook the sound
and climbed the song
until a string
tied to a cloud
we all called home
it moved along
and I held on.

GROWING UP SLOWLY

AUGUST 30, 2005

I've peed on my leg three times this week. The first time was at a department store urinal. The aim caught the bowl just so that it bounced 'round an awkward dip in the backboard, skimmed back across the piss pond, circling right out onto my leg along with... Someone else had already peed in that urinal, and there had been no flush, so... I began to panic. I was not done peeing and had to wait it out while the mix slowly ran down my leg, absorbing into my skin. I zipped up, ran to the sink and gave a good scouring to my shins.

The second (airport) and third (at home) times were even less amusing in the moment. These incidents of bad aim seem to be a clear reflection of my week. I have been throwing down with myself for... well, three decades, but this week felt like Round 16 against Joe Louis on crack, crowd's chuckin' lemons and I'm steady tryin' to box and make lemonade. Knock out's gotta happen soon 'cause I ain't about to dance in circles much longer. I haven't questioned myself so much since the time I played an entire game of Trivial Pursuit alone, pitting 5 different-colored pie holders against one another.

I've started reading "Demian" by Hermann Hesse, but have only gotten through the Foreword and Intro. Already I am reminded of and astounded by Hermann's ability to teach, gracefully. (Side note: The Big Blue. If you've never seen it, go, rent, now. If it's been a while, please, feel, that.)

I signed up for 10-days of silence in October. Vipassana meditation...
I should probably shut up about that.

There are moments of clarity daily. They open me up with a breath and keep me calm. They feed me the answers. And they hold me lovingly. They are gospelstitches. My childish ass has got to let them heal. This feud I'm having with myself isn't even original. But goddamn it is thick and rooted.

Here's to today, slowing down, suspending judgment, and breaststrokes through chaos.

Going, Home

I've been hooked on the word Gospelstitch for quite a while now. At some point on a plane I made a list of my favorite words combined. Watertrain. Gospelstitch. Hungerpunch. Fatherlock. Milkword. Oceanchuck. Windfight. Lipsplitter. I was even gonna name my last CD "Run On Anything" "Gospelstitch" instead.

Ryler Dustin, Anis Mojgani, Tia Fields and I comprised Team Seattle 2006 for National Poetry Slam Finals in Austin. I had been inspired by a quote at the end of the documentary "An Inconvenient Truth" which went something like, "When you pray, move your feet." We all knew we wanted to write a piece about prayer. Ryler had already written most of the first half of the piece when we realized how an excerpt from "Some They Can't Contain" fit perfectly for the second half.

The four of us tied it up, added some tight lines, fine-tuned, but Ryler's consistent ingenuity with words is the key reason it all came together. They've given me their blessing to print our poem. We were such a team. All respect. No bullshit.

If you were to put buddy wakefield gospelstitch *into the YouTube search engine you might find phone camera footage of Team Seattle opening for the National Poetry Slam Team Finals, when my voice completely blew out, but my doofus didn't, and my team had my back so damn good...*

Once finished, I asked the team if we could call the piece "Gospelstitch." The word, for me, had finally been defined by this poem, which holds up well enough on the page as one voice even though it was written for four.

GOSPELSTITCH

I pray thanks
for the woman's heels
I heard on the way here tonight–
they sounded like salt.

When I pray
I pray thanks for the small things,
for flowers and other natural holidays,
for my eight-year-old niece flying her kite
like an umbilical cord.

When I was eight
I prayed for a chest of kites.
Now I pray for You to open
my chest of kites.

Lord, let me write,
leave me autistic and typing
until my windows bust into a thousand silver doves
and I know the poem is done.

And when the words break too much glass inside me
I run when I pray.
I run when I pray on trails
watching the branches blur
to the sun's Holy Sanskrit.
I carry your forests
in my heart.
Your fields
are on my back.
I have not fit your ocean into my chest

yet
but I *have* fit its sound.
Like trees,
like lightning,
our prayers come
from the ground up.

My God's abridged book
is a children's story
where the lessons are simple
and the smiles lift like first grade watercolors.

When I pray
I pray in museums.
I pray over sweat-stained stages.
I pray with vinyl prayer wheels.
I pray by reading math, eating pocket-watches
to suck the chain back to your chest.

You are the men and their saws.
You are silence.
You are gospels.
You are the shoulders of a woman
whose name I never learned.
You are the fire returned back to itself
with every
burnt
book.

When we pray
our chests peel back
like open love letters the size of tide,
the way tide sounds

when it crashes your tympanum,
the way tympanum sounds
when it turns the word *eardrum* into a cymbal.
We play percussion when we pray.
We sing when we pray.
We laugh when we pray.

When I pray I move my feet
for the goosebump
in the heartbeat...

And I drop my jaw at fire when it's flyin' out my eyes, Lord
I plunge my coiling wires in the water till I rise
above frogs
and pop rocks
and boxes
of roof tops
and the noises I can't outrun
even when I'm running twice the speed of sound already
and three times the speed of my blood

'cause everybody's got voices
and everybody's got some they can't contain
like my need to be redeemed
at any time
in any place.

So you can bring on your boogieman loading his fuss
and gunning his fattening desire
'cause we've got bees on flowers
with honey on hold
for those made of gold
but wrapped in wires

who keep themselves inspired
by the way they feel their spines
screaming, sparkling gods
who gotta live by the way they shine.

And this is not a dot-to-dot plot
or a battle on your god
of the makers of money (odd mockers of drum)
who all peel and staple great gobs of large labels
to a god they just wanna slum.

No,
this is *my* time and place.
This is *me* saving *my* saved face.
So if my heart starts to radiate bold broken glass,
y'all,

relax…

it always pumps this fast.

So get thee behind me blindness
and come to me quietly light.
Our god loves people like poems,
loves poems like prayers,
and loves prayers even when they are silent.

We pray until our words run out,

and Yours

linger

still.

*And then there was Team Seattle 2007's group performance piece written by
Ryler Dustin, Danny Sherrard, Tara Hardy, Corbin Bugni and me.
I'm not gonna color-code the lines with who says what,
to avoid distraction. Though strange, the poem reads well enough
without breaking down whose voice is supposed to go where.
We only had three meetings before National Finals.
The four core members of the team felt like it'd be a cryin' shame
to not take the opportunity to write a piece together.*

*Danny (who writes about the swing set chains in this poem, and ended up win-
ning the 2007 Individual National Poetry Slam Finals) wanted to do a collabora-
tion based on the last lines of a song I wrote twelve years ago called "My Point
Forever Endlessly." When Ryler threw down his 1-minute piece from the World
Finals, all our eyes got big and excited and we started building. I'm pretty proud
of everyone in equal parts for writing this piece, committing it to memory, getting
it blocked and ready to roll out in about 12 hours.*

*Though Corbin Bugni of Youth Speaks Seattle was not on our team, we were all so
enamored by his line "break into my prayer" that we used it. It's just too good to
ignore, especially comin' outta the gullet of a 16-year-old.*

WHEN THE TRAIN CAME

I have come here from the guardrails.
They call me Sparky...
because I send sparks... off the guard... rai...
uhhm – rails. Listen, I'm not entirely comfortable being human.

They say laughter is the best medicine
so I wrapped my arms up in swing set chains
just to see if I still have funny bones
I do.
They are aching now

like a foot
lost to a trap.
I've paid for these legs with my mother.
As soon as my stalk was long enough, I ran.
And though it is good to be here with you tonight
I'm still running.

Take a left
at the saw mill of my vicious doubt
and meet me behind the orphanage of my voice box -
we are building you a poem.
It's a boat shaped like a piano
and it'll carry us away like a lullaby
on the sky's slow river. Listen,
we all get to leave something behind,
like the guardrails
and the chains
and the traps
like the fact that my dad left my sister
two minutes after she was born

like I was born: guilty, and kicking, and nervous
and some say our mothers were already gone -
but we are building them a poem
and it's got room for all you people
so jump in, hold the edges,
this is a high-powered mutherfucker
with duel fuel intake dulcimers
and a string quartet spoiler on the back.
I'm almost done.

Someone toss me the Holy knuckles
of a blue collar worker,
and that photo of a baby
upside down in the womb
I can slap to the front like a title page.

Yeah,
go ahead,
break into my prayer

because some of us -
some of us are on fire for the answer

still catching it
and releasing it

because somewhere
somewhere along the fault lines
lies the preposterous idea that we forgive ourselves

and this boat,
this is how I know we're gonna make it

and when we do

because we will

tell me my brothers will forgive us for kicking to the surface of the sea.

Tell me I can stop punishing my legs for being stalks
upon which to leave the wound that made me.

Tell me that from now on there will be doctors to hold every newborn
like it was their own broken wrist.

Tell me that when these swing set chains untie themselves from my arms
I won't just point at my chest and say no one lives in here.

Tell me my heart beats a war drum
that my eyes are not just armies

but my spine
is a harpoon.

Tell me it's a full moon at high noon
and I'm squaring up my driest devils
with the song of a monsoon.

Tell me I won't lie the next time I see myself.

Tell me this isn't the last time I see myself.

Tell me we'll glance once out these side-view metaphors
before we lift off, cast up the funeral kites
for everyone we thought we lost
and want to get back to again –

I promise,
I will leave everything before I leave you.

So sister tell the choir to hurry up
with that voicebox and *the orphanage*

'cause where we're goin,' people move so fast
they never leave each other behind

and everyone speaks like my arms want to speak to you,
like the highway speaks

…openly…

…And I remember seein' 'em break and run off by themselves
and I remember they were full force in song
throwin' their bodies around like wands
and I remember – clearly – they wanted out.

And I remember when the train came
they all hopped it
though they never claimed to ride that way
but it was midnight
and it was goin' to Georgia
and it was free.

...IN THEM ALSO THE FUTURE SWUNG.
JANUARY 24, 2006

Jamie DeWolf (formerly Jamie Kennedy) of The Suicide Kings was two seats away from me at San Quentin State Prison, smiling like a shark, looking for a bucket, or a saucer, or somethin' to catch my eyeballs with.

I get a little nervous before every performance. This one was no different, except that I was in prison.

We were being protected by a chubby guard boy with a mustache dressed in all green who I coulda knocked out with a pencil.

There wasn't a mic to keep me centered, or to manipulate my voice.

It was a Slam. They were gonna tell me what they thought of me immediately.

I knew I was gonna stick my landing, but there's always that possibility of sharting or burping up dinner in the middle of a performance. The thought stalks me endlessly. Embarrassing moments are not shy about giving themselves unto me.

Most of the nervousness was in my need to say something meaningful without preaching geek, without stutter-stepping the nonverbal vibration I know I'm capable of, to say the good stuff with grit, and awareness. I was so eager to remind them how high the volume can go, how much more we can release our beasts through vulnerability.

The better half of me was pretty comfortable with the fact that I was about to open up my nerve endings to an oversized classroom stuffed with a hundred-and-fifty prisoners who were spilling out into the hall and adjacent rooms. I just wish my eyes could've been a little less telling for the people sitting next to me, and that my blood would've learned to tap sixteenth notes without so much racket.

Jamie was losing confidence in me. He couldn't tell if I was gonna buckle under the weight of these energies who bench press burden for a living, or if I was gonna set it off. Jamie's already Slammed in front of these guys a couple times before. Most of the prisoners already know his talent. They already know he shares their bite and their restlessness. They already know he was born on the backside of a switchblade needle, that he's been infected with those who came before him. They relate to Jamie. He's cut with venom, raw with glory. He's a teeth eater too. They know Jamie can hold his own when it comes to game face. They relate to him just fine. If you know Jamie, you know what I'm talkin' about. He reveals it in his first impressions.

I, on the other hand, hold these traits somewhere on the inside. I don't play that instrument so loudly. I sing those black & blues in the shower, or on long drives by myself. I map it out on the page for months where it usually heals itself then breathes. I get no credit for being immediately threatening. It is not in my person to harsh you first, not without apologizing if I do.

I was pretty surprised that only three performance poets from the Bay Area found the sack to toe up, come out and rip it. Granted, a few of the Bay Area poets weren't allowed because of warrants or records, but what an incredible opportunity lost for the others. I mean, it's San Quentin.

I was even more surprised to find out that the four of us who did show up wouldn't be carrying the Slam on our shoulders. Two of the prisoners (Chu and Abdul) hosted, and about 10 of the prisoners actually Slammed alongside Jamie, Geoff Trenchard, Kiria (?; powerful female voice from Berkeley) and me.

After a short open mic with about five prisoners, Geoff Trenchard had the unenviable first position in the Slam and had to warm 'em up. Geoff's also been there before. He's also in The Suicide Kings. The prisoners know they can trust Geoff, too. He nailed it. The guy is an amazing writer/performer.

The room was surprisingly respectful. In fact, those men came proper with much respect, not afraid to shout out when they were feelin' it. My kinda crowd. But still... was I their kinda crowd? I knew I was, but they didn't.

Jamie stepped out of his comfort zone and read a new piece on page. They've seen his other works. It was phenomenal, as usual. Even on page that guy knows how to uproot a tree. He got a 29.5 out of 30 from the judges/prisoners.

Now, granted, we all know that a Slam's just a gimmick to involve the crowd in a spoken word show. In most situations we stopped caring about arbitrary scores a long time ago. But something about being in that prison... I gave a shit what they thought, even through their scores. Universality is incredibly important to me. What most folks consider the bottom of the barrel is a huge part of that universal reach. I needed to know we weren't so far apart.

The prisoners weren't bad poets at all. There were a couple of them who locked my eyelids back by the way they used hope in their swing. Two of them got perfect 30s from their peers.

There were lots of poems about Tookie Williams, the former Crip-turned-children's-book-author who was recently executed amidst *much* protest.

I was slated to perform fourth-to-last.

There was a prisoner who really wanted to read before some bell rung. He was indignant and frustrated like they were gonna run out of food before he ate, or the bus was gonna leave and not care to wait for him. So they put him ahead of me. I didn't care. It's not like I was gonna argue.

The bell rang and a fourth of the room cleared out. I was a little deflated. I wanted all their ears. In the frenetic moment of prisoners heading back to their cells, the inexperienced hosts skipped my name and moved on. The organizer reminded the hosts to throw me in the mix. Then there was small confusion because the only two people left to perform were both named Buddy. Finally, with an exhausted breath, the host just said, "Alright, Wakefield's up," to choppy applause.

I dangled in front of them like cartoon steak for cartoon dogs, eyes ripe and ready.

I could feel their urge to nudge each other and laugh at my easy targets, my weakness for smiling.

In an instant I found the first words of *Guitar Repair Woman* and spoke from the gut:

"My mother told me, 'If you ever become a rock star
DO NOT smash the guitar.
There are too many poor kids out there
who have nothin'
and they see that shit
when all they wanna do is play that thing.
Boy, you better let 'em play.'"

They liked that, and everything about the room said "RIP IT."

So I did.

Their eyes got bigger than mine. They had no idea I was gonna swing like that. Man, it felt good. Really good.

29.9.

There was a second round I didn't know was comin.'
They took the Top 5 of us.
It was three prisoners, Jamie and I.

It was a beautiful moment to walk back to the front of the room with the prisoners yellin' "Bud! Buddy!" Boy that felt good. So much mutual respect for the intention.

I did "The Information Man."

In the part where I say how the info guy is "juggling predictable conversation with folks who look like iceberg lettuce and who believe that the flat lines of small talk will give us life," I pointed to the guard involuntarily. He was dressed all in green. Thank goodness for synchronicity 'cause that mufugger looked just like a big ol' ball of no-nutrient lettuce and everybody there felt it even more when the next line let loose: "I want them to leave." They all laughed.

There were two truly releasing moments the prisoners got and embraced:

"If you've never been rocked back by the presence of purpose
this poem is too soon for you.
Return to your mediocrity
plug it into an amplifier
and rrrre-think yerself!"

And

"Even at your worst, you are fucking incredible."

Van Morrison would've been proud.
There was so much energy in the room.
There was such movement.
I want you to know the movement.

To see tears of solid hope in a caged man's eyes... Thank goodness.

30.0.

I wasn't the only one. There was delivery after delivery from prisoners and Jamie that rocked the place; damn near took the roof off. The guard couldn't keep from smiling every so often.

After the show we got to shake hands with the inmates and talk heartfelt, without fear, for just a moment.

The prisoners were rushed out of the room, and were gone.

We were also rushed off a minute later.
I was the first to sign out.

Without thinking or questioning or looking I left the room and walked out into "the yard" by myself.

I looked up. No guards, just *lots* of prisoners stone cold. Some of them have had nothing to do but work out for many years. They were not in conversation. They were not cheering for the Slam any longer. They had returned to their game faces, leaning, arms crossed, staring, sizing me up. All eyes were directly on me.

I imagined they were asking themselves how the little poet would react to an immediate realization that he was walking directly into a hundred prisoners alone. I imagined they thought I would turn around and go back inside. I wanted to. It was too late. I couldn't turn my back on 'em like they were animals now that the show was over, once I did my tiny little job for a few minutes where I pretended I was some sort of lasting light.

I did not stop walking toward them, and they did not give any welcoming gestures or smiles, so I said in my coolest funny man, "The fuck? I don't want any trouble."

It was like watching the icicles on one entire side of a house drop at the same time. They completely broke game face and laughed again. I strolled up next to them, suddenly so welcoming and interested. I did not wish to be center of attention whatsoever in this situation, so I focused all my conversation on one man who shook my hand with spark in his eyes. I spoke in a tone that did not invite everyone to listen. There were handshake interruptions and they made my night. It felt good. I felt myself tearing up, then immediately steamrolled the idea of becoming emotional.

Man, I wanted to listen all night. Now I ain't sayin' I could make it on the inside of that place by any stretch. Not at all. That's not something I need to prove to myself. I'm just sayin' I wanted to spend the night and hang out with the fellas, hear their stories, redirect their excuses, remind them what they're good at, hold a mirror on reality and run circles around the dumb shit the mean people in their lives have offered them.

Yeah, I know, like that's gonna happen.

Eventually the others were all signed out and the last bell rang, and the animals walked slowly back to their cages in one big scattered pack.

Jamie and Geoff were eye to eye with me, smiling. Incredible. I said I wanted a beer, but not too loud. They probably miss having a beer with a friend.

Lights Out, Dufresne

GUITAR REPAIR WOMAN

My mother told me,
"If you ever become a rock star
don't smash the guitar.
There are too many poor kids out there who have nothin'
and they see that shit
when all they wanna do is play that thing.
Boy, you better let 'em play."

Okay, if she ever starts in on one of these lectures
your best bet is to pull up a chair, Chief
'cause Momma don't deal in the abridged version.

She worries about me so much some days
it feels like I'm watching windshield wipers
on high speed
during a light sprinkle
and I gotta tell 'er, "Ma,
yer makin' me nervous."

She was born to be laid back, y'all, I swear,
but some of us were brought up in households
where *carefree*
is a stick of gum
and the only option for getting out
is to walk faster.
The woman
can run
in high heels
backwards
while double-checking my homework,
bursting my bubble,

rolling enough pennies
to make sure that I have lunch money,
and preparing for a meeting at my school
on her only day off
so she can tell Miss Goss the music teacher,
"If you ever touch my boy again, big lady,
I'll bounce a hammer off your skull."

I remember her doing these things swiftly and with a smile
in her discounted thrift store business suits
that she wore just bright and distinguished enough
to cover up the 30 years of highway scars
truckin' through her spine.
Some accidents you don't need to see, Rubbernecker.
Keep movin'
'cause she made it.
She's alive
and she's famous.

We can stretch Van Gogh paintings
from Kilgore, TX to Binghamton, NY
and you still won't find the brilliant brush strokes it takes
to be a single mother sacrificing
the best part of her dreams
to raise a baby boy who – on most days –
she probably wants to strangle.

We disagree *a lot*.
For instance, she still thinks it's okay
to carry on a conversation full throttle
at 7 a.m.
whereas I think…
Oh, wait, no that's right…

I *don't* think at seven in the morning!

But we both agree that *love*
makes no mistakes.
So at night time,
when she's winding down and I'm still writing books
about how to get comfortable in this skin she gave me,
I see rock stars on stages
smashing guitars
and it is then when I wanna find 'em a comfortable chair,
get 'em a snack,
and introduce them to daylight:

This is my mother,
Tresa B. Olsen,
Runner of the Tight Shift,
Taker of the Temperature,
Leaver of the Light On,
Lover of the Underdog,
Mover of the Mountain,
Winner of the Good Life
Keeper of the
Hope
Chest,
Guitar
Repair
Woman.

And I am her son,
Buddy Wakefield.
I play a tricked-out electric pen,
thanks to the makers of music and metaphor,
but I do my best to keep the words in check,

and I use a padded microphone
so I don't hurt you,
because sometimes I smash things,
and I don't ever wanna let 'er down.

SUDDEN MOVEMENT
NOVEMBER 02, 2005

"This will also change."

Prior to the 10 days of noble silence there was registration.
Out of minor concern for the bald guy being unaware for 10 days, I let him know there were two hairs he must've missed while shaving his head. In a couple of hours no one would be able to tell him, so I did. He said he had Alopecia, a hair loss disease, and his hair was beginning to grow back in again. Then he stood at different angles of light so I could see there were other stragglers, not just two. His name was Dan.

I nodded to a guy named Oliver Klomp who was walking past me on the road to the parking lot, but I was hesitant and redneck about the nod. Oliver just stared at me. He shined a little. Okay, a lot. He was like the kid from the movie "Powder" only not so pasty. Confident enigma. In my head I accused him of trying to be someone I tried to be once... In college I spent an entire semester force-feeding a quiet guy phase so people would find me tortured and mysterious. I wish it weren't true. This time I would start my silence when it became required, when I would surrender my entire self to someone else's teachings (S.N. Goenka) for over 10 days.

Oliver Klomp. His name, it's too good, I know. His person is even better. I knew it was his name because I heard him register. "Oliver Klomp, with a K. K-l-o-m-p."

I was already agitated. The place was awkward, like a funeral. Nobody knew whether to talk or look down or put their hands in their pockets or put their hands in their armpits and make fart noise songs. Maybe it was just me. We arrived at 2:30pm and the orientation didn't begin until 6pm. I walked to my car in a distant lot that couldn't be seen from the main house. I listened to Beck's new CD, track 10, and tried to find one last cigarette under the seat somewhere. By no means am I proud of it, but I've smoked off & on (mostly on) for 17 years. I found no cigarette. The morning of October 19th was my last one. Hopefully, I'll be able to say that twenty years from now.

I'd watched 6 episodes of South Park the night before we (me and the three strangers I volunteered to pick up) arrived. Cartman's voice was still tumbling through my head, helping me to deal with the anxiety. My pretend Tourette's Syndrome was begging to bust loose already. Cartman continued to make me giggle for the rest of my stay. Specifically, because of the episode where he goes on a talk show as an out-of-control teen, waves his chubby little hand around and keeps saying, *"I do what I want."*

Vipassana exceeded all expectations, literally. There were 11 hours of meditation daily, 7 hours for sleep, 2 hours of random breaks, a one-hour discourse with Goenka (extraordinary daylight man), and 3 hours for meals (breakfast, lunch, then some fruit at 5pm). The retreats are held in international locations and are free. Really. The healing was immense, the vibrations did not shrink back, the teachings have no time for words, and I'm not gonna spend all my energy here convincing you. Most of it is for me to savor. I've kinda just been excited to share the funny parts, and the people, and the synchronicity. Telling you what went on inside me and where it took me... I'm not the guy who can give you all that at once.

"Liberation can be gained only by practice, never by mere discussion."

There were things about meditation I did not foresee. The gas. For sure the gas. The personalities of gas. Gas's ability to sound like a talking person. Burps. Michael A. Michael A's burps were constant and bass (though there was a bass-collecting process he accessed which was fairly gross). I kept mine pretty silent. No, seriously, I did. There were a couple times the burp came out sloppified, like I was a baby with an oopsie, but for the most part I was graceful about the burping.

A majority of the farting was from Michael A. He made no qualms about his wind. In fact, I got the feeling he assumed everyone would just embrace his constant wind.

On Day 5 or 6, when he rolled back in his bed to use a rocking technique to expel all his gas, quite loudly, in our room, I became noticeably cranky. When he did it again the next day, he was fully aware of my disapproval.

But the farts and burps were not the most disruptive gases. Stomach growling easily trumped them. Like on the first morning when Leon (my stomach) spoke about 17 different vulgar languages, with hits like:
- Climb the Colon
- Squeaky Toy
- Stomach Acid Ricochet
- Gargle Squeeze
- The Dying Baby Remix
- Start the Car Medley
- Slosh Heave
- Torture Chamber: A History of Painful Sounds, Volumes 1-3
- Pierce the Belly
- Throw Your Voice
and
- Amplified Oatmeal

Not since Ms. Roden's Pre-Pre-Algebra class in the 7th grade have I realized how vocal Leon can be, not until I was shut in a room of utter silence with 60 other people. He awoke the first full morning at 4am with fury. So did the dust mites, which I'm allergic to. When Leon wasn't squealing through the lips of a balloon, I was sneezing. I had to walk out of meditation hall that first morning and meditate in our room (nine of us lived in the room) until the group sitting at 8am.

When I stood up to remove myself, fabric softener fell out of the blanket and my feet cracked loudly all the way to the door as I walked. My feet have cracked ever since I was a kid. When we lived in Chaparral Village, also in the 7th grade, I hated how my mother's room was next to the kitchen because I could not sneak in for unhealthy snacks without her hearing me.

I am an embarrassing moments magnet.
I'll tell you the rest later. There is still so much to share, but I must go now.
Subtle Sensations, Change
www.dhamma.org (Dhamma means Law of Nature)
Click on "worldwide course schedules" and go.

GOENKAJI AND THE GONG PEOPLE
DECEMBER 13, 2005

In the ten full and two half days at Northwest Vipassana Center, there came a streamline of details through my senses which rose and fell away with such consistency and clarity that I began to truly experience the now as my life, not just some unachievable goal.

Around Day 4, I began identifying which of my eight roommates was approaching our sliding glass bedroom entrance by the sound he made on the gravel path leading back from meditation hall.

Jacob was easiest to identify because he walked so fast and frantic that it made the gravel path sound like a dog trying to open a bag of potato chips.

Ankur made slow strides but was only noticeable when he wore shoes. Most days he didn't wear shoes.

Matthew walked like a man on his way to work at a job he liked. He pulled doors open the same way.

For much of the twelve hours we spent in meditation each day, there was the option to meditate in our rooms. Although most students preferred sitting among the energy of the whole retreat in meditation hall, I felt best at ease in our bedroom. There was always the off chance I could be alone there (you know, maybe vibrate right outta this world with no one watching).

By the way, we promised not to masturbate or have any sexual activity for the entire stay and I kept my promise. It wasn't so hard... step off my pun.

Jacob and Nate also mostly chose the relentless solitude of our bedroom. Jacob could have his Tourette's Syndrome tic fest and Nate could sit, legs outstretched, hanging his long feet (in their warm and patterned socks) off the bunk above me.

Nate was pretty stealth with the gravel, and considerate, and mannerly, with the sub-textual hints of any good church boy... Book covers are amazing illusions.

Shiloh took messy steps and would no doubt come into the room making some sloppy noise like a heavy exhale cough, or kick his shoes off against the wall. He frequently triggered Eric Cartman from South Park to go off in my head: "Goddamned hippie!" But I had to like him because I saw him as the perfect partner for my dear friend Shona.

Others would typically wander back from meditation hall and join us in the room, one by one, within a half-hour to an hour after the start of each session. There was no dependable routine for who would show up first, or who would choose the room and who would choose the hall. Sometimes I stayed in the hall for group energy guidance, but mostly I conducted self-surgery from that spot on my bed, away from the camp at large.

Michael A walked heaviest and most unaware of the noise sharp rocks can churn out. I also worried Michael A might kill the fuzzy black & amber caterpillars with his thoughtful thoughtlessness. The caterpillars sometimes had to cross the gravel to get to greener grass, I guess. I imagined the caterpillars had already worked out some sort of Michael A alerting system with one another to try and get off the gravel in time, but black & amber caterpillars aren't so fast.

Arun was only a little less lead-foot than Michael A, but was more considerate with his door-opening and -closing techniques, so for those two I sometimes had to wait until I heard the way the door got handled before I could tell who was who.

Oliver Klomp made no sound at all... Okay, a couple times, but it's way more fun to continue believing he's a total enigma.

When footsteps on the gravel path sounded unfamiliar to me, I knew they were the steps of seekers staying in the rooms next door or across the yard, all "old students."

Among those old students not in our room was an older man who resembled an agitated version of Santa Claus.

The bathroom had three showers, two toilets and a urinal. Everything but the urinal had a privacy curtain, which was a cloth on a rod. Even though the privacy cloth was pulled shut, I could always tell when Santa was peeing because he completely dropped trou. I mean the guy would pull his pants all the way down to the ankles the way real young boys do before learning common laws of efficiency. It made me brainchuckle every time.

Once, while exiting the toilet area, I pulled the curtain back too fast and took the whole rod down with it. Oliver Klomp was standing still on the other side, waiting to use the bathroom. We – both a little startled – held back knee-jerk laughter and moved on. It was the first time I saw Oliver as real.

There were interrupting cows and bi-polar cats and itches I did not scratch. There were volunteers and dirt bikers gone wild and specifically changing landscapes. There was toaster patience. There were wet grass walking areas, puddles on benches, nights lined up star-fog-star-fog like boy-girl.

And there was the gong, in a sacred wooden frame planted firmly in the walking area near the front of meditation hall. It had little hand-held brothers & sisters who were kept somewhere out of sight, but the great gong itself was alive and dutiful and did its whole job without fail. Its keeper was named Alex.

Alex was the assistant to the teacher who sounded the gong to wake us up, to tell us it was time to take rest for the night, before and after every meal, before and after every meditation, before and after short breaks.

Alex lived in a room that was built inside of our room...
"If someone's motive is only to serve, how would the question arise of gaining respect, power or reputation?" –S.N. Goenka, Dharmasringa Vipassana Centre, Nepal, June 26, 1994

Every time I think I'm near the end of this story, I remember how complete it felt to be there and so I just keep typing. I'll have to get to the synchronicity soon, and Goenkaji. *[Note: many Vipassana-related journal entries were written which are not included in this book.]*

Electric Blessing, Circle Jockey
www.dhamma.org
P.S. I mentioned "relentless solitude" in this entry. We're not done talking about that.

SPIRITUALIZED

DECEMBER 16, 2005

Nate, on the bunk above me, was usually still awake. The two of us were – as far as I could tell from his big gapes of breath and sigh – always the last to fall asleep. Sometimes we would both pull one quick breath at the same time to smother a chuckle when things got out of control with Jacob's default tic or the sleep talkers.

On Night 5, as I lay awake in bed, again, long after the sleep talkers had harfed out the bulk of their sentence fragments or English accents for the evening, and soon after Nate had finally fallen out, I began to crave tacos.

Crunchy taco shells, juicy marinated meat, shredded cheese, diced tomatoes... warm crunchy taco folds, dripping marinated meat yums, melted cheese ropes, fresh ripe tomatoes... zesty marinated awesome sauce bits of tender meat traveled by strands of melted cheese gods cupped by sweet red tomato shovels in a buttery shell of crisp warm corn toast... aaaahhhHHHH! AAAAAHHHHHHHHHGGG!!

"No new sankharas [craving]."
Goenkaji repeated it daily and often.
"Remain equanimous."
"Work diligently."
"Remain aware."
"You are bound to be successful."
"Craving and aversion will only cause you misery."

Every night for one hour, Goenka would speak to us via pre-recorded video discourse. Although it seems a bit impersonal at first thought, Goenka transcends stigma with his pure and penetrating wisdom. During the discourses he would tell good-spirited stories and elaborate on the process we were then encountering with so much trust, making sense of our internal progress. Beyond the poignant insight, he is a surprisingly funny guy, Goenka.

Sometimes during meditation he would guide us with statements like the ones above. There is something to be said about the impact of voice when it comes from a man at peace with himself.

In the very first discourse on Day 1, Goenka's wife is shown sitting next to him on the video. She looks like a pile of comfortable blankets. Her presence is absolute stoic. If someone like me were to look too closely at her, they might think she's a bit miserable. I worried about her personal peace. Book covers...

In the first discourse on the first day, the camera eventually zooms in on Goenka only. It does not show his wife again until Day 10. Other than some throat clearings, she remains quiet throughout the videotaped discourses.

"No new sankharas."
"Stay equanimous."
"Work diligently."
"Remain aware."
"You are bound to be successful."
"Craving and aversion will only cause you misery."

By this point in the retreat, I had finally understood that my thickly-accented friend, Goenkaji, was saying "aversion," not "abortion," and so I listened to his wise reminders. They replayed easily through my memory that night in bed as I tuned out a river of thoughts leading to an ocean of piping hot tacos, and I went to sleep.

Mexican hovercraft.

***

Each morning, in the lobby of meditation hall on the information board, there were posted any changes to the daily routine. Always, though, in the top middle of the board display was written the day. DAY 6.

Day 6 was moving along with depth and progress just like any other healing day goes at any other given Vipassana center in any other part of the world at any given moment.

Unless I were to peg specific memory notes in my brain to remind me of something that happened on a specific day, it's hard to tell which events happened on which day because of the general timelessness enveloping our retreat. But I do remember that I craved tacos on Night 5 and that I rounded the corner for our last meal of the day at 11am on Day 6 to find, right before my very popped and lighted eyes (like sunrays beaming from the heavens through a break in the clouds)...

Tacos.

GIT OUTTA HERE!

I was beside myself inside myself.

It was the first time I had really yearned to speak during the retreat. I felt as if my chest would burst open, and that I would proudly exclaim with an enriched voice, through powerful lungs, "You are all welcome! Everyone, please enjoy these tacos which I made manifest."

But I didn't.
I just ate them.
The meat was tofu and the shells weren't so crunchy as I had imagined, but there were tacos. That night, Night 6, as I lay awake reeling from the day, I wondered what vegetarian dish I could possibly make manifest next.
Vegetarian lasagna for sure!
Maybe if I just focused long enough on it...

For the 11am meal on Day 7, I walked falsely confident into the dining area with high hopes of seeing vegetarian lasagna, but...

There were potatoes. Potatoes with Indian spices and other things I need not recount. It was the second time I'd wanted to speak at the retreat. I wanted to verbally double check with the kitchen volunteers to make sure they hadn't forgotten to set out the lasagna I had made manifest the night before in bed.

There was no vegetarian lasagna. My shoddy psychic ability, as with dozens of other instances throughout the years, had merely come and gone of its own volition; rising then falling away simple as any other sensation.

There was *Let It Ride, Festin,* and the recurring two of clubs. There was the lightning in Pinehurst, Year of the Monkey, and the feather in Amsterdam from the cover of Illusions by Richard Bach. There was Lillian Laverne Montgomery. Psychic experiences have been steadily woven into my world a blessed number of times throughout my tiny history. These moments – as in a quote I read about life somewhere – are not a puzzle to be solved, but a mystery to be lived. Just savor them when they happen. Call them coincidence. Call them synchronicity. Call them anything you want but, at the very least, savor them. And don't enter them into a story swap. Extra sensory perception recounts lead to the most dishonest and uncomfortable conversations, especially when said conversations happen among people who are desperate to believe in anything other than themselves. I tend to end up feeling like there is a one-upping that happens in these conversations, as if grade school boys are talking about fist fights.

***

On Day 10, during the last group sit before our noble silence ended, there was singing from Goenkaji. His comforting voice is the exact cross between an ancient man in the forest and a relaxed child on a pillow. His singing is – to say the least – *adorable* in the way it embraces off-kilter. The way he would enter our ears with sudden assurances, exiting with his low motor drag, Goenka purposefully rocked the healing mic.

Note that sometimes I call him Goenka, and sometimes I call him Goenkaji.

I have not researched or asked for reasons behind why some do or don't add the "ji" to the end of his name. I think "ji" signifies that he is a very special teacher, not just a name, but I could be a very mistaken student about that.

So on Day 10, as Goenkaji warmed our hearts with chanting and song during that final sit before we – the entire camp (both men and women) – left meditation hall to converse in common areas, I did sensation sweeps over and through my body.

My spirit joined in with my brain joined in with my body joined in with my blood joined in with my cells joined in with my atoms joined in with my dreams joined in with my frames joined in with my chaos joined in with my visuals of the fizzling sankharas and subtleties rising to the surface then passing away, cleaning out, cleansing, letting go, simultaneous.

It was during this uncommon flood of whole power that I completed my memory goal and added the 100th peg in my head (a memory technique I'd been perfecting throughout the retreat). Internal scanning finally became clear to me (the piercing and penetrating instruction I'd misunderstood on Day 9). I was able to sit the duration comfortably without experiencing back pain, or needing to adjust my sleepy legs. I heard the missing links my new CD needs in order to deliver. Synchronicity was comin' like a waterfall and I was mouth agape underneath it, arms open and cry smiling inside the moment anthems are built from. The kind of anthem I was feeling can not be sold to a nation. It really can only be worked for continuously, and lived.

During this last group sit on Day 10, before "noble chatter" would be allowed to swallow the silence, I found peace with Michael A. I conquered a bout with hay fever. I understood my entire life's outcome, and achieved happiness, and loved entirely, and... Goenka suddenly returned from the hour-long silence he had left with the room.

He chanted and sang to give us a clean ending.

.

It was a fresh song he fell into, one I did not recognize from any of the previous days. It was more harmonious than the others and it leveled all doubt. That's when his wife joined in, flawless and assured. Her voice was of the same world as his, crossing between ancient woman and relaxed child. There was a celebration of synchronicity all around me, and no one said a word, or moved a muscle, or even sniffed.

As the brilliant voice combination between Goenka and his wife rose and fell away, the teachers at the front of the room exited. Deep breaths abounded. Footsteps sprinkled the room. The door behind me opened and closed many times as students made their peace and left meditation hall.

When it was finally time, my body opened its eyes and stood up.

There were five or six students still in the hall who would see themselves to a clearing before following the rest of us outside.

I pushed open the door of meditation hall into a typical northwest sun.

Cool breeze washed over me.

Conversations were already pounding into one another from a distance.

I kept my head down and leaned slightly into a nice walk. I did not desire talk. The times in my life when I have felt so complete can be counted on one hand.

Synchronicity continued to reveal its constant presence in my life.

Judgment rose and fell away as I heard the words of others in conversation scattered around me:

"Oh, yeah, you're just like me."

"I really want to stick with it this time."

"Have you ever heard of Ken Wilbur?"

Alex, the perfect assistant teacher with his gentle presence and clumsy gong technique, sounded the tune that signaled the serve of our 11am meal. I continued my walk, though.

I took the longest route on the path in the back walking area. Even the realization that I would not always feel so complete could not penetrate. In fact, it was the first time I ever was so high with no disdain for coming down, realizing I had finally found my answer; that hope carries over easy into fruition when we use the right eyes.

Coming down is not a pain which demands reaction.

After walking in equanimity around the worn path, I headed for our dining facility to face the talking retreat, take a seat, and eat a delicious lunch.

I nearly crumbled from the joy (like certain kinds of cheeses do) when I rounded the corner and saw it there, perfectly baked, golden holy grail, still hot for me... vegetarian lasagna.

There Was A Scar Here, Floodlight Face.

IT WAS A WOODPECKER

DECEMBER 27, 2005

In telling the story, outside of these journal entries, of my time at Northwest Vipassana Center to friends, I have stated how my first words at the end of the 10-day silence were, "It was a woodpecker."

It's good first words. But after more thoughtful reflection, as I sit here recalling other events from that day, I've come to doubt myself. I don't remember what my first words were for certain. I'm juggling an order of instances. I pulled the woodpecker account up from an entire day that lasted one moment; a moment made up of dozens of wholes arranged in my head more like flowers than some line of files.

As I stood looking up, eyes fixed on the trees carrying psychic conversations in a continuum, Ankur strolled toward me, barefoot. I looked over quickly, silence broken, and we locked eyes. There was a sort of hilarious exchange of smiles before we looked back down to avoid intentionally breaking the silence. It was a big moment for no other reason than the fact that everything seemed so highlighted.

I was happy to tell Ankur, at lunch on Day 10, as I prepared my plate of vegetarian lasagna, that it was a woodpecker. I was hanging out in those trees with a woodpecker, a woodpecker that was not pecking wood because it was hanging out with me.

"It was a woodpecker," but I am not confident it was my first words.

Throughout the 10 days, I noticed several of the men at the retreat wearing the same distinctive pair of rubber boots, but I passed the coincidence off as though the boots were some common man-item I had never purchased at the secret shop for alpha males. Turns out, all those boots belonged to the center and anyone was welcome to use them. I never took the time to ask for boots. I didn't want to talk unnecessarily. I would wait for special occasions when the sun dried out the thick dew grass so I could go for a walk without soaking my shoes and socks.

On Day 3, the teachers had broken my expectation frame of having those 10 days in my life to be completely silent, because they made me speak to them. Once I got over my anger about being coaxed into speaking, and once it was clear to me that noble silence was not just silence for the sake of silence, but that talking to the teachers or to the assistant teacher, Alex, was important for staying clear in the experience, then I felt at ease to do so.

It should be noted that we were also allowed to speak with kitchen staff, but I never did. Not even when I suspected them of holding out on cookies. I spoke with the teachers when they invited me to speak with them. And I spoke with Alex.

I approached Alex for breathing guidance when my allergy to dust mites made it all but impossible to perform anapana through my nose. I wasn't sure if anapana or Vipassana could productively take place by breathing solely through the mouth. Alex, who has been practicing for eight years, was also the runner of registration, ringer of the gong, man who lived inside the bedroom that was built inside of our bedroom, and the guy who would call for me to see the teacher with an air of humble servant and an air of Addams Family.

When we were allowed to speak again on Day 10 (after the final serious meditation where Goenka's wife helped bring it all home), I stopped Alex to ask how I might score a pair of those boots to keep my feet dry on a walk before lunch.

I had been talking to Alex sporadically like that for the whole retreat. Maybe talking to Alex again didn't much count as my first words. I'm not so sure he was really the first person I talked to on Day 10 anyhow. I'm not so sure it matters what the first thing I said was. At least I'll get to tell you all about Alex.

There was also the quick encounter with Nate and Oliver. I can't remember if that happened before or after I ate lunch and mentioned the woodpecker to Ankur.

Nate and Oliver were together in conversation, headed back from the walking area, just as I was setting out. Everyone was so at ease and kind at the retreat that there was no reason not to break the verbal ice by saying hello to these people I'd been sharing a room and spiritually living with for ten days.

"Hello, Nate. Hello, Oliver."

I said it in a way to keep from spilling all the joy I had bottled up inside.

Oliver could have responded with a full story of his life and I wouldn't have noticed because Nate was so gung-ho to talk!

"Hey, what's your name again?"

"Buddy."

"Hey, Buddy! We were the guys who couldn't sleep, man!"

I smiled and nodded and kept strollin.' Wait, ya know what? This DID happen after lunch when I spoke of the woodpecker to Ankur because I remember my first vocal impression of Nate was also in the dining area. He had said "Howdy!" as he walked by, then we both laughed at how loud it came out.

Don't lemme give off the impression Nate was a big stuffed country bumpkin. He was an athletic kid with charisma; charisma that lay in a gray area between frat boy charm and one who is charming in the way he beats up frat boys.

When we later had our own conversation on a bench, Nate used the word "fuck" (or forms thereof) at least two dozen times to express himself fully. An old high school friend had fuckin' talked him into coming. He had the same twisted front tooth and innocent tone of voice as an old best friend of mine. He fuckin' lays tile, man. He wants to be a fuckin' professional fuckin' Frisbee golf player. There are $100,000 tournaments. He liked the Vipassana experience. He's gonna see if any of it [magically] fuckin' sticks in his everyday life.

Nate was one of the calmest meditating presences in our room. That now seems strange to me.

Nope, my conversation with Nate and Oliver was not my first words, either. It wasn't to Alex about the boots or to Ankur about the woodpecker or to the stray cat who loved love on the path.

We're having a moment right now...

Listen, I was gonna use the forgetfulness regarding my first words as a tool in this journal entry to tell you about holons (wholes within a whole), or maybe a continuum, or maybe more moments that I had with Alex and Nate and Oliver and Dan and Michael A. But I'll tell you about all that good stuff later because while writing this entry I have absolutely remembered for certain what my first words were.

When I left meditation hall that day, Day 10, to go for an amazing walk with synchronicity, not ready to speak with anyone yet, respectfully keeping my head down as a nonverbal cue so no one would interrupt the electricity I was exploring; soon after Goenka and his wife trailed out with that hypnotic song; as I suspended all judgment building up toward conversations whirling around me, and before walking the black & amber caterpillar path leading to vegetarian lasagna, I stopped by the room to have a pee.

To get to the bathroom, we first had to take off our shoes, switch into our slippers, then walk through the bedroom.

As I entered the sliding glass door to our bedroom, Oliver Klomp, who was adjusting his sweater and heading out, looked over to me, smiling, and said something very similar to (if not exactly), "Did you enjoy yourself?"

Without meaning to, I answered him in much the same way Jennifer Jason Leigh's boyfriend from the movie "Georgia" would have answered him...

"Very much so."

CON.TIN.U.UM n.

1. a link between two things, or a continuous series of things, that blend into each other so gradually and seamlessly that it is impossible to say where one becomes the next

2. a set of real numbers between any two of which a third can always be found, and in which there are no gaps

Born, Frequently

GEORGIA
JUNE 10, 2006

"What goes up
just might float away.
What you're sure will leave
might stay." -- Amy Steinberg (Wide Sky Life)

Oliver Klomp was conceived under an olive tree in Egypt.
Turns out, Oliver is something of a poet too. And a musician.
A good musician.
He handed me a CD before we left the Northwest Vipassana Center in Ethel, WA.
The CD was the first from Oval League (www.ovalleague.com), a band he created.
A good band.
The second track is entitled "Relentless Solitude".
It's a ghost singer's song, comes alive when no one's lookin.'

There are storm clouds in big flat pushy Texas.
They get tall and roll over into bruise colors,
build speed and run dark notions with the wind,
like sparks off the guardrail.
I can feel the thunder fatten up from as far away as Georgia,
see the clouds truck in like a train
swallowed by a tunnel vision
ascending.
There are no mountains here to split the truth,
just plains to stretch it
so far
it fits.
It shuts me up.
The pets get twisted.
Cats lose cool.

Eyes
dart.
It's my turn to guard the dog now.
We kept a horse named Andy once.
I'd imagine Andy in the stables
with his eyes rolled back in his head.

Even when the downpour happens, the ground goes bright green here
in Texas,
where I grew up.
Could be the radiation.
Could be the God on it.
When that kind of sky comes toward me I feel right about being haunted.
The good side of haunted, when it rumbles fully towards me, open magnet, breathing,
when I'm aware of the slips of space between my shirt and my skin.
It's the same reason I like ghost stories and nightmares,
for the goose bump
in the heart beat.
It's the same way I fill up with Georgia.

This is what I know of Georgia:

The first song I remember hearing when my [real] dad died was "Midnight Train
to Georgia" at 17th Street Pub in Huntsville, TX. I started crying. There was a
stand-up bass player named Ben telling me a story. Ben didn't know about my dad
dying. When I got up slow and walked out of the pub, Ben hollered after me that
he was sorry. He thought he was telling me a really bad story.

I saw "The Night the Lights Went Out in Georgia" on HBO when me & HBO
were still children.
I was the legal son of Bill Stevens then.
My name and dad were different.

I don't remember what the movie was about, but there was a lot of lonesome and dust and a song by the same name. It went,
"That's the night that the lights went out in Georgia.
That's the day they hung an innocent man.
So don't trust your soul to no back woods southern lawyer
because the judge in the town's got blood stains on his hands."
I remember a man in that movie near dead in a pickup truck on an open dirt road in the hot sun with the door open, a body falling out, and an overwhelming depression. Boarded-up buildings in humid backroad southern towns make me feel the same way.
If Bill Stevens is still alive I bet he lives with a similar atmosphere in his gut.
Do I wish for that?
Only when I'm not okay.

The closest my [real] dad and I ever came to bonding was through music.
Specifically, "Georgia on a Fast Train." Billy Joe Shaver. In my dorm room.
One of the sexiest women I ever saw was in that video.
If I were to continue talking in superlatives about sexiest-evers, I would tell you to see the underplayed "Spacelord" video by Monster Magnet.
And ARL in a ball cap.

From "The Information Man:"
"If you pull a bent breath
through the second hole of a harmonica
tuned to the key of Georgia
while a train moves by
on the tail end of dusk
there's a good chance
you will finally know
what it means
to rest.
I
have not yet rested.

It takes a long time to make love with someone who hates themselves."

"I know our shoes were stitched from songs about highways.
Best songs are the ones about Georgia
even though I've never been there.
It's the only place I still believe in Jesus."

Georgia carries the last sentiment in "Some They Can't Contain," and a stretch of
presence through the end of "A Stretch of Presence:"

"...and I remember seein 'em break and run off by themselves
and I remember they were full force in song
throwin' their bodies around like wands
and I remember clearly
they wanted out.
...and I remember when the train came
they all hopped it
though they never claimed to ride that way
but it was midnight
and it was goin' to Georgia
and it was free."

Atlanta's own Pastor Creflo Dollar laid healing hands on my head once when he
came through Houston.
I fell back and pretended to be saved.
Carried myself out on a truth stretcher.
Fuckhead.

Until two weeks ago I'd never been to Georgia other than the Atlanta airport.
Finally I got to go, to perform there.

The venue may as well have been the inside of a giant freight car,
not just because I inflate the truth with my own life,

but because it really did pull out and smoke up like a giant freight car
with a full bar inside of it might.

The crowd was friends, intimate, ready to roll, till the wheels fall off.
The organizers and the show in Atlanta were perfect.
I got to do something there that I always wanted to do in a Georgia venue, ever
since I saw the movie "Georgia." Before my last piece, "The Information Man,"
I spoke the name "Conrad." If you were in the room, and you remember that
moment, it's the only time I left you.

Thank you, Karen and Theresa and the folks who drove all the way out, and the
guy walkin' the pig on a leash, and the audiences, and Remond Heart Holder, for
letting me have that.

A dream fog man used to walk into my room and paralyze me till I choked
on lucid. If he had rolled in that night to show me death again, I woulda died
willingly, and cool with it.

Hermann Hesse died alone at age 85 of a cerebral hemorrhage.
Goddamn brain exploded in his sleep.

"Hesse never wrote to preach. He was trying to find a way out of the madness he
found himself in. His books are not inspirational, but are more like a record of his
own attempt at understanding." --username Dionysus

I don't wanna go down like Hermann did, focusing on focusing on focusing on
focusing on focusing so far completely till the details run through me like a needle
axe over and over.

"...Siddhartha was for him the beginning of the search for something pure and
universal. But he failed. Hesse realized that in order to truly achieve the purity that
he was seeking, he needed not just an intellectual understanding of the world, but
an existential commitment as well, a complete reversal of his own life, a drastic
change to the way the simple things in his everyday life are negotiated. That step,

a leap of faith, really was, and still is for many of us, a terrifying step to take. Intellectually, Hesse knew what he had to do. Existentially, he could not commit..."
--username Dionysus

It is written on my spine to be better than that.

I played reverend last week.
The night before the wedding rehearsal dinner I got a call from my good friend Joe telling me our good friend Jon (the producer of "A Stretch of Presence" and "Run On Anything") was headed to the hospital with his wife...

BABY!!!

WELCOME TO THE WORLD MIA LOUISA BERARDI!!! !!!

The water had broken.
Less than an hour later, my good friend Seth called to say that our good friend, Dave,
the groom, his mom just died. Wow.
Dave's mom died.
Two days before his wedding.
That took a minute to sink in.
When I told good friend and groomsman Jim, he said he was going to hang up the phone and stare at the wall for a minute.

They would go ahead with the wedding.
Thick skin party.
Handled with care.
And Love.
I congratulate you on more than being married, Dave.
Your strength was incredible to witness, and support.

It's safe to say I was a bi-polar reverend, battling tears every time a reference to Dave's mom came up in the ceremony, then chuckling to near uncontrollable at the under-breath groom-side mumbles.

On game day, before the ceremony, I wanted to harf up the lump in my throat and step on it. Most of my old college buddies were there; a room full of smart asses who've all seen me make my f-ugliest party fouls and bad choices.
It was as nervous as I get.
It's been 9 years since I graduated college.
Did my heart a lot of good to kick it with those guys again.
A lot of good.

Both sides of my mom and stepdad's family came over to celebrate the birthdays of my stepbrother (Jeff) and me. We swam in the canal with Jeff's friends and my cousin's kids. We fished and ate barbeque. It was beautiful to be with my cousins, and my ma, and family, and all those leftovers.   be a bright,
bright, sun-shiny day.

I'm finally back in Seattle for the summer.
Thank goodness gracious.
Seattle summers are the payoff for all that winter rain.
It was a long season of touring and being away from home.
Rain is my lucky number, but only when I need luck.
More rest now, less everything else.
For a long time.
Blank paper.
New direction.
Cue muse.

The first track on the new CD is called "Healing Hermann Hesse."
Oliver Klomp gave us permission to sample "Relentless Solitude" for this track.
It hits me like the good side of haunted by storm,
which is to say Georgia,
which is to say death,
or birth,
and commitment.

With many thanks to the precious crew in Savannah, and the incredible Florida venues, for the moment.

On My Mind, George

It should be noted that the following poem was originally 3 to 4 tremendously heavy pages in length, and was written to more than Hermann. In fact, it was not originally for Hermann, but was for general relative entities and called "The Un-Numb of Milkword Gospelstitch." I cut it down considerably, focused, and renamed it for inclusion on my CD "Run On Anything."

I've pieced parts of it back together for this book. I did not properly save the original. Some of the lines may be familiar. I ended up using them to complete important thoughts in other poems. Showing you this may also reveal, more than usual, that most of what I write are notes to myself. Maybe now's also the best time to state that "Notes to Myself: My Struggle to Become a Person" by Hugh Prather was the first book that opened my eyes to what Van Morrison or A.J. Whipple or God might call the eternal now.

HEALING HERMAN HESSE

Hermann wants to eat nicotine
sometimes.
He asks
for a lot.
He paces space to make himself nervous
because some people are better at surviving than living.
If you wanna get heavy
he'll teach you.
He knows it.
Spends his time falling from the weight.
Got a lead brain.
It's a battle magnet.
He carries it around by the guilt straps.
Don't laugh.
You didn't see the size of the blizzard that birthed him.
Fits of snow.
Cotton rocks.
Whipped white bullet stretches
pinned with chips of teeth
to his habit of crying for help.
He doesn't land well. Hates landing.
It reminds him of not living up.

Listen, I know there were days you wanted to die

when the sky was so clear
you'd stand obnoxious underneath it
begging for stars to shoot you
just so you could feel at home.

I know about the ways you misplaced all the right words,

stockpiled every important social cue you ever missed
from the first time you learned you were wrong,
waited to make it right
once everyone stopped watching.

I know you let them beat up your beauty in bed
because redemption was still alive in you, howling relentless, gathering strength.
Felt like ecstasy when they pounded it out of you in the hard dark.
Those days of dead weather
got all strung together
and they spoke for you,
wore you down to telling everyone here it was a good life
so you could run back into the wails of your windfight.

I know the parts of your past that haunt you the most
are the days you weren't being yourself,
and I know that's why most of your past haunts you.
There were so many who found you out,
and they were right.
You were good.

So
un-
numb.

It's now ya gotta quit it, Milkworder
Mr. Self Murder.
Hiding is not an option for giants this good at showing up.
You show up.
It is okay that you showed up missing.
We've all abused ourselves then looked over the wrong shoulder about it.
Call it fatherlock.
You were picked like this.

I know it still feels right when the song shows teeth,
when the movie shows prison,
when there's the chance of a sky split open.
I know you've still got the hate inside.
Don't wanna hurt nobody.

I know the nights you believed someone would come for you,
take you out of here,
when the weight of those empty pockets and your ugly reflection
ate holes through the grip they told you to get
while you were being pulled under.
You know about being pulled under.

And I know it makes ya say things you just don't mean
like *DIE mutherfuckers!*
DIE DIE mutherfuckers!
Hold tight if I love ya
'cause it might not last long.

I know you hate hope
because it's the hope that makes you stay
and it's the stay that's got you down,
but you stay so far off the ground.

Hermann will not bow down
to gravity.

Falling, he catches up to himself mid-air
just before the ground smacks.
Pullthroat,
they call 'im,
Sharpturner.
Nothing touches the ground here.
Ground is at capacity.

He sees that.
He falls back.
He patches parachutes together with a kite knife.
It's big enough to raise him in the updrafts
where he hides himself away in the angles of air
outlined by his knack for believing
that this life

it's gonna work itself out.

ARICKA FOREMAN'S SIGNATURE
JANUARY 9, 2007

"Religion is for people who are afraid of going to hell. Spirituality is for people who have already been there." --Northern Sun

Remond Liesting is responsible for teaching me that happiness is more than just a reduction in suffering.

Tracie Moran gets all the credit for calling us "brutally beautiful."

Mike Dillon is responsible for "drug of choice = more," "reading people's skin," and "fix it."

I wrote this piece in full in my head while at Vipassana Oct. 26- Nov. 5. This is the first time it's seen the page (November 15, 2006).

HUMAN THE DEATH DANCE

On the face of her phone
Wileen programs a message to herself
so that when the alarm clock rings
the screen flashes:
EVERY DAY IS ONE DAY LESS.
EVERY DAY IS ONE DAY LESS.
For some people
happiness…
it's just a reduction in suffering.

Like Jordan.
Jordan tattoos the words
FORGIVE ME
in thick black letters
down the inside of his arm
so that when he looks at his wrist
he will remember to not hate himself so much.
What he keeps forgetting
is that there is life after survival.

After Dave left
Mary started sticking her face
between the film projector
and the movie screen
so that when the credits roll
she still gets to be somebody.

When Tara's past comes back
she mashes chalk into the sidewalk
until her knuckles bleed.
She scribbles and scrapes

scribbles and scrapes
until the words take shape
and this is what they say
they say *I wanna die mutherfuckers*
die DIE mutherfuckers
hold tight if I love ya
cause it might not last long.

Y'all, we're all gonna die.
That's the exciting part.
It's learning how to live for a living,
that's the tricky stitch.
Just ask Denise
whose family taught her when she came into this world
that *family* equals *love*
so Denise took that shit seriously
but after a lifetime of craving acceptance from their cruelty
she now finds herself jamming Polaroid pictures of these people into her typewriter
and pounding out the last letter of the word *mercy*
over and over again.
She strikes the key Y.
Y? Y? Y?Y?Y?!

And the answer?
The answer comes in the form of a handwritten letter from the moon
says,
This is brutally beautiful.
So are we.
This is endless.
So are we.
We can heal *this*.
Signed,
Crater Face

P.S. See me for who I am.
We've got work to do.

But my father
he didn't read moon
he didn't speak moon
and he didn't write moon
so there was no letter found next to his body in the garage
when he chose to leave this world on purpose
without telling us where he was goin' or why.
There are still days you can catch me
tape-recording eternal silence
and playing it backwards for an empty room
just so I can listen to his dying wish
shhh.

Yes
it's true.
And the apple,
it doesn't fall too far from the tree.
But thank goodness my family tree
was in an orchard on a hill
that rolled me to the river,
and that river
ripped me through the rapids,
and those rapids
rushed me into this moment
right here
right now
with you
at the mouth.

Y'all, this is my church.
And if church is a house of healing...

Hallelujah.
Welcome.
Come on in.
As you are.
Have a look around.

Stay out of my porn.

There are massive stacks of bad choices in my backyard.
Clearly I have not yet reached enlightenment
beyond a few fleeting moments
but I'm tryin'
and I found somethin' here I want ya to have.
It ain't much
just a story
but it's all I've got
so take it.

It's called *Dillon*.

Dillon's drug of choice was more
so he took more and more
until the day he woke up babbling
in a pool of his own traffic jam
realizing he was killing off the best parts of himself
and claiming he could read people's skin.
When Dillon looked down at his heart flap
it read, *Boy, go find your spine*
and ride it outta here.

Wileen's gut said *Day 1*.
Jordan's arms were **FULLY FORGIVEN.**
Mary's face:
The

Endless.
Tara's knuckles: *Healing.*
Denise's fingertip said *C?*
C. C. C.C.C!

And my smile,
Dillon said my smile it said *Fix it*
so I came back here to the mouth of the river
to look at my own reflection under the moonlight
and see what it says for myself
where down my whole body
it is written
P.S.
See me for who I am.
We've got work to do.

As for Crater Face
I can't speak for him.
His skin
is a brutally beautiful
handwritten letter
from the sun.

Originally, "Human the Death Dance" was a series of images and concepts I'd memorized while I was supposed to be meditating during my second stay at the Northwest Vipassana Center. Once it was mentally cut & pasted and edited and combed through, revised countless times and finally completed, I realized that many of the original visuals and outcomes intended for "Human the Death Dance" never made it into the poem.

"The Art of Die Smilingly" is a follow-up to "Human the Death Dance" in that it revolves around the original first step in my journey to write "Human the Death Dance." The only original image still not included in either piece involves some sort of strange show-and-tell I imagined having with my old stuffed animals. Meaning, the stuffed animals were gonna show and tell me revelations. And even though I don't own a stuffed rabbit, I still pictured one telling me how half moons resemble tacos, and that night he ate three tacos. Now he is stuffed with moon.

For my father.

THE ART OF DIE SMILINGLY

If you really want this to be your last day on Earth
on purpose
and there will be children
who are yours
and you will be leaving them
permanently
please
before you go and
take away Mother Nature's chance
to translate you proper-
ly listen –

Right now
with no doubts
head out
hire hard-working
lovers of life
who really need the money.
They may be difficult to find
but they are worth it.
Pay them well.

They will build you the world's largest neon sign
somewhere around the size
of a souped-up, sideways
40-story waterslide. Please,
if you don't have the money
steal it
from someone who kills people with it.
If you get busted
fuck it

it's not like you had better plans.

When the neon sign is finished
don't tell anyone what you are doing.
You do not need to leave a note.

The hard-working lovers of life
will hang your sign from the deepest edge
of the Grandest Canyon
where you will wait until dawn
for stillness
and the low
down
fog.

Now, duck away into that.
There'll be a rocket pack.
Pick it up.
Strap it to your back.
Dry your eyes.
Feel around on the ground
for the metal, beaded pull string
leading to the neon sign.

Hold it in your hand
tightly.
Say a thank you
to anything,
then run,
fast as you can
for the gravity.

Don't think
just jump

up
and outward.

then quick
flip the switch to the booster pack,
pull the string
to light the sign,
open wide
your open eyes
and hang on tight to the lifting
because you *will* shoot up and outward
as the neon writes its light through the night
in cursive tubes of waterslides
hung high and tight on the canyon side, says,

"DON'T WORRY KIDS
THE MOON WILL CATCH ME"

There'll be a fiery blast
in the eyes of the workers watching.

There'll be dust spreading out
like a helicopter castle when it's landing.
But you're leaving.

There'll be your children below
in awe of you, waiting, and wondering,
"What are you doing?"

And there'll be one last thing: the parachute,
take it.

'Cause I've got a mountain of battle scars in a meat wagon

I been haulin' around like a memory
healing my rough edges in the holy pull of gravity
comin' from a neon runway back to Earth
willing to bet that if you'll just cool your jets
long enough to drop the rocket act
maybe you'll feel the glory in why everything keeps
pulling on you relentless, towing you all the way back home.
It wants you to stay.

So power off.
Fall into it.
Fall any way you want to,
but ya gotta tug the ripcord firm from your chest
if you're ever gonna keep from dyin'.
The saving of yourself
(and the way those straps will jam your nuts
straight up into your hollow parts)
is jarring.

Look around on the way back down.

You're not the only piece of patchwork
birds can pull worms from.

If I were the man in the moon
and my eyes were a little better
I'd just barely be able to sound out the words
stretched across the top of your parachute
written by the lovers of life
who are very good with signs like,

*"DON'T WORRY MOON
THE KIDS WILL CATCH ME."*

WREST
APRIL 17, 2006

"The winner of the rat race
is a rat." - ?

Before the first full day of meditation started, there was a day of checking in and getting situated and Formica countertops and thin crust carpet and durable white plastic patio chairs inside. Shoes came off at the door.

I like being on time.
I'm good for it.
Showed up at the beginning.
I went for a long walk in the field while folks trickled in and registered.

There was a black-and-white cat who greeted me in the field as if to say,
"You're on the right path. Now you must pet me until I can take petting no more."
So I pet him.
A lot.

That night, during the greeting session, we were asked not to pet the cats.
They come from neighboring properties.

We were to practice noble silence and maintain equanimity without distraction.

Throughout the 10 days, I steered clear of the little guy.
I did not give him a name.
It was a cat.
Staley, probably.

I watched a woman succumb to the pressure of the purr and pet him somewhere between Days 6 and 9. She petted him real good for two quick strokes then re-focused. I wanted to run across the path and the yard, arms up and arched, fingers curly, screaming, "PET THE KITTY!"

I took a deep breath instead.

There was another cat with no interest in people. She sported borderline mange and walked with the urgency of Snuffalufagus on tranquilizers. She maintained equanimity and had no desire to be cuddled. She was at least 127 years old in cat years, best I could tell. She was also in no mood to have psychic communication with me. There were several black & amber caterpillars and a woodpecker who were into it, though. We totally connected.

***

I believed in Santa Claus till somewhere around the second grade. There was consequence for not believing in Santa. No gifts. Exposing the Easter Bunny and other lies followed suit. The Tooth Fairy fooled me for at least three teeth to my recollection. For my first 23 years, I was scared into believing in a God who would eventually and literally burn forever anyone who did not strictly adhere to His laws as written by man in a book using language that has long since been subtly mutilated.

There was my stepsister who stole from the offering plate, who lied more than she spoke. There was my aunt who lost both her legs and most of her family to the lies she soaked in. There was my dad and the reasons he chose to close the garage door and turn the ignition. There was the fraud of my former employer on Gig Harbor, and the millions of dollars he stole, and the mountains of hope he crushed just by lying. There were the days I lied about loving this place.

When I was 24 I worked with a family who were completely prepared for Y2K. They had a house in the middle of Nowhere, Eastern Washington, and a thoughtful paper packet packed with loads of useful information and expectations. I was to consider the packet an invitation. I coulda stayed with them through Armageddon if I wanted. There were documents and "evidence" and I was convinced, even went so far as to warn my closest friends (one of whom has still not lemme live it down).

I've believed in more twisted individuals and entities and selves than I could ever wanna recollect tonight; people and notions whose teachings I planted inside of me only to yield mediocrity, if not thorn, if not cactus, if not fly trap, poison bite, teeth grinder. Sawdust pulls up the stink.

My beliefs have cried wolf more times than I care to remember. I do not type this without a rise in temperature or a little embarrassment. Each time I get fooled I have the exact same dialogue with myself. It goes like this:

"Buddy, do NOT stop trusting people."

Then back, "I won't."

If I lose trust in people, what's that say about how I view myself?
A pretty grim reflection.

So in the welcome session on the first night, when the catalyst of this international Vipassana retreat, S.N. Goenka, stated on paper his expectations of us, including surrendering our entire selves for 10 days to the teachings of Vipassana meditation, my internal dialogue went:

"WATCH OUT, BUDDY!"

Then back, "No shit."

I know where I stand now, especially when the ground gives way.

***

Alex (the man who lived inside a room which was built inside the room where 9 others of us lived) has been practicing Vipassana meditation for over eight years. His eyes are big and curious and shy and welcoming. His clothes hang like burlap sacks. It is easy to want to hug him, not too tight, because he is aiming for love.

Plus, physical contact is not allowed.

I was glad to eat lasagna with Alex on the last day. We were both glad. I clearly got a lot out of Vipassana and wanted to know more about his life. I asked if he lived at the center full time and if he considers himself a monk. He let out a bent breath to show being tickled. He told me he had a job at a food co-op and a significant other, a home and... we shared a genuinely great meal. Toward the end of it my eyes filled with water. My eyes interrupt.

"So this is it, isn't it? I mean, this is the answer."

I wasn't really asking.
Alex saw my eyes briefly and knew the feeling of sanctuary (comes like salvation). I was experiencing it. He also knows that feeling will fall away and return as many times as I'll let it for the rest of my life as long as I'm able to simply observe the law of nature exactly for what it is. He saw that I understand how to live it and own it. He saw that I know where peace with my self rests. He saw a kid so sweetly situated in the first time, a first kind of extended stay inside.

Kids run off.

Alex knows about the come-down for those of us practiced in landslides.
I could tell.
Didn't matter. I was experiencing the answer.
I experience the answer.
I am my own answer,
a complete unit,
not so divided like all the contrasted chatter bangin' out from the inside
(distractions; passing particles I just suspend and focus on; tiny parts of the whole).
We are our own whole answer.
There's a way to come clean.
Maybe that's obvious,
especially to the dirtiest among us,
but talking it and practicing it are two different things
rooted in different places.
Lately I have felt rooted in different places.

***

On Day 10, once we were welcomed to speak again, after lasagna lunch with Alex, I went to the room shared between nine of us. I laid down in my bottom bunk craving nothing, certain of the coming gong that would invite us to one last sit with the group in meditation hall. Michael A was the only other person in the room as I lay there.

It's been a while since I've had a chance to tell more of the Vipassana story. In case you don't remember Michael A or don't feel like reading the old entries to catch up, maybe it'll help jog your memory to know he was The Leader of the Gas. Gashopper. Master Blaster. He lived in the su-burps. The Big Burper. Burposaurus Rex. Wyatt Burp. He was like the air tube in an aquarium. There was an endless river of gas wheezing and blowing and hurtling out of him. His actions were always loud and late and slammy and stompy and I experienced angry thoughts toward Michael A.

I made my first attempt to quell the anger on Day 9 when Michael A sneezed in meditation hall. I sat a tissue next to his cushion as a sign of care. I sensed his surprise. He'd been noticing my rude. He had brought out the rude in me a few times. I have a tendency to reflect the very thing driving me crazy. Much of the time it's safe to call that "passive aggression." It's a fairly tasteless human trait. I'm embarrassed by how much I've used it in my lifetime.

As I lay on my bed, silent despite the end of the noble silence, Michael A sat straight up on the edge of his own bed, putting socks on, not making the verbal contact I'd been hearing him make with others. He didn't feel welcome around me. I had already kept my head low in passing him before lunch. He knew I didn't want to speak with him. But, in fairness, I was keeping my head low because I didn't want to speak with anyone yet, not just him.

At any rate it was time to accept our met paths.
I couldn't leave the Vipassana experience without acknowledging his presence sincerely...

"On Night 2, you stood up while you were sleeping and goochie goochie gooed the guy in the bed next to you." These were my first words to Michael A.

"I did what?"

"On Night 2, you stood up while you were sleeping and leaned over to Arun and looked at him and goochie goochie gooed him, just like he was a baby."

Michael A laughed. We had a good conversation. He did most of the talking. In the first five minutes he made a Crystal Gayle reference and accidentally imitated a pirate. I liked that a lot. It was a hard life for him. He was already upset with himself for talking so much that day. He's gonna have a crack at being a photographer. I listened.

I really like to listen when I remember to.

***

Recently I dreamt that Remond fixed the garage behind the house where I grew up (from first through sixth grade). The garage was about to fall over on itself last I saw it. I was gonna take Re and show him the tree next to the cornfields where, as a child, I would sit and make things up and no one knew where I was. When I got back to the garage, Re was fixing it. If I had known how to do it I would have done it, but I didn't. So Re did. He was happy to be fixing it. Then he fixed the broken crops and they grew over the hills-were-green up to a sculpted gravel path. Dark spot. Turn back. Stay a while. It's being fixed. Trees sprouted. Then Remond fixed the broken house. He painted it, too. He painted everything around me. Stealth. The whole town I grew up in finally felt happy. I woke up happy. I really like waking up happy.

***

I've been slacking on the journal here. I don't like it to feel gratuitous or like an item from a to-do list 6 billion miles long, and the truth is that I've been sorta burnt out on exposing myself, so I've been waiting for a good moment to share.

I kinda just wanna go into the turtle shell with a typewriter for a minute.

"If I am lost it's only for a little while." -B. Bridwell

Upstroke, The Mange Cat

Lotta people been askin' about the voice on "The Information Man" from my CD
Run on Anything. *It's Mack Dennis.*

Mack Dennis is a performance poet and storyteller born in New Orleans, raised by his grandparents, Clothilde and August Jasmin. He started out working in the cane fields of the Laura Plantation. He moved to New Orleans in 1960 where he lived with his mother, Cora Johnson. He experienced the Civil Rights movement firsthand in The Big Easy, joining up with the freedom marchers and becoming New Orleans's first black bus driver. Three years, a wife and three kids later, he was a member of the Black Panthers, who socialized in a shotgun house on Foy Street, which led Mack to the state penitentiary at Angola. Having driven a taxi-cab in San Francisco for the past 25 years, he's been around the block a few times. I'm honored and blessed to have his presence on my CD, Run On Anything, *as The Information Man.*

Amen, Student
P.S. Thank you for the indigo you gave us.

THE INFORMATON MAN

After over 300,000 miles,
12-dozen breakdowns nervous,
one too many midnights
and a *bunch* of broken laws later,
I have come here from out of the rain
and into this rest area
caught 22 miles between you and me,
watching the information man
behind his information booth
juggling predictable conversation
with folks who look like iceberg lettuce
and who believe that somehow
the flat lines of small talk will give us life.
I want them to leave,
like a big deal orchestra removing itself from the stringed section
so I can fiddle with fate and make music.

There is a distance the size of bravery.
It forms like words in the mouth of a baby reaching out
for the point where all things meet.
On one end of it sits an information man
who I imagine holds down his second job as church bartender
behind locked doors leading to a bell tower
we will never get to see.

At the other end of this space
I am standing like shoe polish on an overstocked shelf
hoping that one day someone will pick me to make things better.
This is not a showdown or a shootout
We are not facing off.
But I can feel the rumble between dusk and dawn

as if the chance to come clean with myself
will be outlawed
unless I relax.

I have heard
that if you pull a bent breath
through the second hole of a harmonica
tuned to the key of Georgia
while a train moves by
on the tail end of dusk
there is a good chance
you will finally know
what it means
to rest.
I
have not yet rested.

It takes a long time to make love
with someone who hates themselves.

It feels like I've been standing here
for exactly that long

when, at last,
the rain outside drops off
and takes everyone in this rest area with it
except for me, and the information man.

If we were created in God's image
then when God was a child
He smushed fire ants with His finger tips
and avoided tough questions.
There are ways around being the go-to person,
even for ourselves,

but today I will get the answer
and you *know* what I'm talking about.
THEE answer.
Emphasis on EE answer.

So I put my best foot forward
and take the kind of deep breath
that gives me away
as someone who deals with anxiety
and odd numbers
every other
other every minute.
In between it
the information man's eyes grab me
then *shift*
back & forth,
like mopping floors
with the sweat I sweat
in battles against myself.
He's got me locked in and is smiling.

If you've never been rocked back
by the presence of purpose
this poem
is too soon for you.
Return to your mediocrity
plug it into an amplifier
and re-think yourself.
Because some of us are on fire for the answer.
I am ready for rejection
and rebirthing balance in my stutter steps
when the info guy finally pipes up
like C.R. Avery on a piano box
and says to me:

Listen,
if I didn't have so much of this life all wrong
I would have gotten it right by now.
I talk a whole bunch
but I really only know a few things
so I'm not saying to follow along verbatim here.
I'll just tell ya the things I tell myself
the things I know
and you can see what sticks...

I know our shoes were stitched from songs about highways.
The best songs are the ones about Georgia
even though I've never been there.
It's the only place I still believe in Jesus.

I know that no matter what it is you believe in,
you gotta spare yourself the futility of making fun of God
because that guy hasn't even talked in like...

ever.

I know troubleshooting yourself in the foot
and acting as center of your own universe
is a tricky dichotomy to deal with
but, yes, you ARE the center of the universe.
If you weren't
you wouldn't be here.

So as the middle of space and everything floating in it
it is your job to know that the emptiness
is just emptiness,
that the stars
are stars,
and that the flying rocks –
fucking hurt.

So please, stop inviting all these walls
into wide open spaces.

I know everything is out there.
It's why they call it everything.

I know there are times
you will lay your head to rest
you will have a moment of brilliance that grows
into a perfect order of words,
but you're gonna fall asleep instead of painting them down on paper.
When you wake up
you will have forgotten the idea completely
and miss it like a front tooth
but at least you know how to recognize moments of brilliance
because even at your worst
you are fucking incredible.
It comes honest.

So return to yourself,
even if you're already there,
because no matter where you go
or how hard you try
or what you do
the only person you're ever gonna get to be,
and I know it,
thank
God is you.

CPSIA information can be obtained at www.ICGtesting.com
Printed in the USA
LVOW090029070312

271894LV00003B/7/P